ONE POT
SPANISH

Penelope Casas

A Sellers Publishing/Madison Press Book

Published by Sellers Publishing, Inc.
P.O. Box 818, Portland, Maine 04104
For ordering information:
(800) 625-3386 toll free
(207) 772-6814 fax

Visit our Web site: www.sellerspublishing.com
E-mail: rsp@rsvp.com

President and Publisher: Ronnie Sellers
Publishing Director: Robin Haywood
Senior Editor: Megan Hiller

ISBN 13: 978-1-4162-0530-2

Library of Congress Control Number: 2008934050
10 9 8 7 6 5 4 3 2 1

Text, cover, design and compilation
©2009 The Madison Press Limited
Recipe text © 2009 Penelope Casas

Produced by
Madison Press Books
1000 Yonge Street, Suite 303
Toronto, ON
M4W 2K2
madisonpressbooks.com

Printed in China by SNP Leefung

Contents

Introduction

When I first visited Spain several decades ago, I immediately fell in love with the country's cuisine. Over the years, as I traveled to every region of Spain and delved into lesser-known regional cooking, my admiration for Spanish cooking grew, and I am still constantly amazed by the wonders produced with a minimum of ingredients.

Although today Spanish cooking has gone upscale and is in the forefront of creative cooking, to me, it is still the epitome of one-pot meals and hearty, down-to-earth peasant cooking. In fact, the national dish of Spain is *cocido*, a hearty meal in a pot with chickpeas and meats, that is found in regional variations all over the country (who would think that a simple potato stew, enlivened with little more than Spanish smoked paprika and a few pork ribs, could be so delicious and memorable?). And of course, what could be more spectacular than paella—the ultimate one-pot meal—so festive, colorful, and crowd pleasing, and made in its own unique pan.

Spanish cooking is based on healthy Mediterranean ingredients like olive oil, garlic, beans, and fresh fish; it also makes use of luscious Iberian ham, chorizo sausage, saffron, and peppers, both smoky and sweet, that lend a haunting flavor to sauces and stews. The Spanish are never without a mortar and pestle to prepare these native ingredients, which are often simmered in primitive earthenware casseroles called *cazuelas* to extract maximum flavor. Spain is surrounded by the sea, and naturally some great seafood medleys, such as Basque marmitako and Catalan suquet, are high on the list of Spanish meals in a pot.

And let's not forget tapas. These mouth-watering little appetizer dishes of Spain, lovingly prepared and served in casual convivial surroundings, are in a category of their own. One wonderful feature of Spanish cooking is that so many tapas (lovely bean, rice, egg, and vegetable dishes, as well as savory pies) make gorgeous meals, as is obvious in this diverse volume of Spanish one-pot dishes.

The key to Spanish cooking is the verve with which it is prepared and enjoyed. Eating is a national pastime and a social occasion—never to be rushed. And Spanish food is comfort food beyond compare, made with the highest quality and freshest ingredients. Even great Spanish chefs in their leisure time undeniably prefer homespun country cooking. As Spaniards are fond of saying, *"¡Buen Provecho!"*—Good Eating!

—Penelope Casas

Salads

Garbanzos Aliñados Con Alcaparras
Marinated Chickpeas with Capers and Red Pepper

Spaniards adore chickpeas, adding them to salads as well as stews. And although French writer Alexandre Dumas compared chickpeas to "high-caliber bullets," today they are highly esteemed for their nutritional and culinary merits.

Makes 4 servings

- ¼ cup/50 mL extra-virgin olive oil
- 2 tbsp/30 mL thinly sliced Vidalia onion
- 2 tbsp/30 mL seeded and diced red bell pepper (capsicum)
- 2 tbsp/30 mL minced parsley
- 2 tbsp/30 mL red wine vinegar
- 1 tbsp/15 mL drained small capers

- 1 clove garlic, minced
- 2 cups/500 mL drained cooked chickpeas
  Kosher or sea salt
  Freshly ground pepper
- 1 hard-cooked egg yolk, crumbled

Whisk together the olive oil, onion, red pepper, parsley, vinegar, capers, and garlic in a medium serving bowl. Stir in the chickpeas and season with salt and pepper. Let stand for 1 hour at room temperature. Serve sprinkled with the egg yolk. ⬭

Ensalada Xató Con Escarola, Tomate, Anchoa Y Aceituna Negra

Escarole, Tomato, Anchovy, and Black Olive Salad with Xató Dressing

This salad combines typically Catalan ingredients, like dried sweet red pepper and hazelnuts.

Makes 4 servings

10   hazelnuts

2   dried sweet red peppers (*ñoras*), or 1 dried New Mexico chile, stems and seeds removed

4   cloves garlic, coarsely chopped

½   tsp/2 mL sweet paprika, preferably Spanish smoked

Pinch of kosher or sea salt

6   tbsp/90 mL extra-virgin olive oil

2   tbsp/30 mL red wine vinegar

6   cups/1.5 L washed, dried, and torn escarole leaves

24   grape or small cherry tomatoes

18   cured black olives

8   anchovy fillets

6   radishes, thinly sliced

2   tbsp/30 mL minced parsley

To prepare the Xató dressing, preheat the oven to 350°F/180°C. Spread the hazelnuts out on a rimmed baking sheet and toast in the oven for about 5 minutes until fragrant. Meanwhile, soak the dried peppers in a bowl of warm water for about 20 minutes until pliable.

Grind the hazelnuts in a food processor until very finely ground. Scrape the flesh from the peppers and add to the processor, along with the garlic, paprika, and salt. Process until finely minced. With the motor running, slowly pour in the olive oil and vinegar.

Arrange the escarole, tomatoes, olives, anchovies, and radishes on individual salad plates. Spoon the dressing over each portion and sprinkle with parsley. ◌◌◌

Ensalada Al Estilo Moro

Moorish-Style Salad with Cumin and Paprika

Cumin and paprika are two wonderful additions to a salad dressing, an idea that comes from the Moors who controlled southern Spain for many centuries. The dressing is excellent on any green or mixed salad.

Makes 4 servings

2 anchovy fillets, chopped	Freshly ground pepper
1 large clove garlic, minced	4 tsp/20 mL red wine vinegar
1 tbsp/15 mL minced parsley	¼ tsp/1 mL Dijon mustard
¾ tsp/3 mL ground cumin	¼ cup/50 mL extra-virgin olive oil
½ tsp/2 mL sweet paprika, preferably Spanish smoked	4 cups/1 L washed, dried, and torn tender romaine, escarole, chicory leaves, or mesclun
Kosher or sea salt	

Mash the anchovies, garlic, parsley, cumin, paprika, and a pinch each of salt and pepper to a paste in a mortar. Whisk in the vinegar and mustard, then the oil, and season with more salt to taste.

Put the greens in a salad bowl. Add the dressing and toss gently. ∞

Ensalada Del Rocío

Tomato and Pepper Salad with Eggs and Ham

For most of the year El Rocío in southwestern Spain is an unpaved ghost town. It only comes to life seven weeks after Easter, when pilgrims come by the hundreds of thousands to these marshlands of Coto Donaña. They ride through the sands on horseback or in colorful carriages, dressed in flamenco style, dancing and drinking the days and nights away in honor of the Virgin of El Rocío.

Here's a great red pepper salad from that part of Andalucía, and it has the region's quintessential tastes: sun-ripened tomatoes, deep green and brilliantly red peppers, hard-cooked egg, air-cured Iberian ham from the mountains of the province of Huelva, and, of course, celebrated Andalusian extra-virgin olive oil. Each bite transports me to sunny southern Spain.

Makes 4 servings

2 medium red bell peppers (capsicums)	½ tsp/2 mL ground cumin
2 medium green bell peppers (capsicums)	¼ cup/50 mL extra-virgin olive oil
2 large plum (Roma) tomatoes	2 tsp/10 mL mild-flavored white wine vinegar
2 hard-cooked eggs	½ tsp/2 mL dried oregano
Kosher or sea salt	4 oz/120 g very thinly sliced Serrano ham or prosciutto
1 small Vidalia onion, thinly sliced	
1 large clove garlic, minced	

Preheat the oven to 500°F/260°C. Put the red and green peppers and tomatoes in a roasting pan and roast for 30–40 minutes, turning once, until skins are charred. Remove from the oven and put in a deep dish. Cover with foil and let stand for 15 minutes. Peel off the skins, discarding pepper stems and seeds, and chop the peppers and tomatoes coarsely. Stir together in a bowl, then arrange on a serving platter.

Coarsely chop the egg whites and finely chop the yolks. Sprinkle the eggs over the peppers and tomatoes. Season with salt to taste and scatter the onion over the top.

Mash the garlic, cumin, and a pinch of salt to a paste in a mortar. Whisk in the oil, vinegar, and oregano. Drizzle the dressing over the salad. Drape the ham slices on top and serve at room temperature. ⬱

Espárragos A La Riojana

White Asparagus Salad with Piquillo Peppers, Egg, and Anchovy

This salad combines La Rioja's celebrated white asparagus with its succulent tomatoes and sweet red peppers in a wonderful dressing that also includes anchovies and finely chopped hard-cooked egg. Ideal for asparagus, the dressing is also tasty on a green salad. Piquillos are slightly hot red peppers that are roasted and packed in jars or cans.

Makes 4 servings

2   drained piquillo peppers or 1 pimiento, chopped

1   small tomato, peeled, halved, and seeded

3   anchovy fillets, chopped

1   tbsp/15 mL mild-flavored white wine vinegar

1   tbsp/15 mL extra-virgin olive oil

¼   tsp/1 mL Dijon mustard

Kosher or sea salt

Freshly ground pepper

1   lb/500 g trimmed, cooked, and cooled thick white asparagus spears

1   hard-cooked egg, finely chopped

1   tbsp/15 mL minced parsley

Put the piquillo peppers, tomato, anchovies, vinegar, oil, mustard, and salt and pepper to taste in a food processor and process until smooth.

Arrange the asparagus on individual salad plates. Drizzle about 1 tbsp/15 mL dressing over each portion of asparagus. Sprinkle with the egg and parsley and serve at room temperature. ⬤⬤⬤

Ensalada De Pimientos Al Estilo Andaluz

Andalusian-Style Red Pepper, Tomato, and Tuna Salad

This version of Andalusian red pepper salad is especially delicious. It includes tuna and green olives, and is served in a bowl with lots of liquid from the peppers and tomatoes. In Andalucía, it is typically an accompaniment to fish fry or grilled jumbo shrimp.

Makes 4 servings

- 6   medium red bell peppers (capsicums)
- 8   oz/225 g good-quality drained canned white meat tuna, preferably Spanish
- 2   medium tomatoes, halved and thinly sliced
- 12 mild bright green olives, such as *gerignolas*
- ½   small Vidalia onion, thinly sliced
- 2   tbsp/30 mL minced parsley

- 2   cloves garlic, minced
- 6   tbsp/90 mL extra-virgin olive oil
- 1   tbsp/15 mL mild-flavored white wine vinegar
- ½   tsp/2 mL granulated sugar
  Kosher or sea salt

Preheat the oven to 500°F/260°C. Put the red peppers in a roasting pan and roast for 30–40 minutes, turning once, until skins are charred. Remove from the oven and put in a deep dish. Cover with foil and let stand for 15 minutes. Peel off the skins, discarding stems and seeds but reserving the juices.

Slice the peppers into ¾-inch/1.5 cm strips and put in a serving bowl with their juices. Break the tuna into chunks and add to the peppers with the tomatoes, olives, onion, parsley, and garlic. Fold in the oil, vinegar, and sugar with a rubber spatula. Season with salt to taste. Cover and refrigerate overnight. Serve cold or at room temperature. ⬤⬤

Escarapuche

Pork Tenderloin and Tomato Salad

I sampled this combination in an out-of-the-way tapas bar in Herrera del Duque in the province of Badajoz, and its simplicity impressed me. It tasted like the epitome of Spain, and I'm sure it's destined to become one of my all-time favorite tapas. The salad also makes a fine main course served with roasted new potatoes.

Makes 6 servings

2 medium tomatoes, chopped	¼ tsp/1 mL dried oregano
½ medium Vidalia onion, thinly sliced	Kosher or sea salt
¼ cup/50 mL extra-virgin olive oil	Freshly ground pepper
2 tbsp/30 mL red wine vinegar	2 pork tenderloins (about ¾ lb/375 g each), cut crosswise into ½-inch/1 cm slices
1 clove garlic, minced	

Gently stir together the tomatoes, onion, oil, vinegar, garlic, oregano, and salt and pepper to taste in a medium bowl. Let stand at room temperature while you prepare the pork.

Grease a ridged grill pan and heat over high heat until very hot. Grill the pork slices, in batches if necessary, for 3–4 minutes, turning once, until browned on both sides and just cooked.

Arrange the pork slices on a serving platter and spoon the tomato salad over them. ⬭

Soups

Ajo Blanco Malagueño

Málaga-Style White Gazpacho

Before tomatoes were brought to Spain from America, this creamy white gazpacho, based on Spain's plentiful almonds, was standard summer fare. Both nourishing and refreshing, gazpacho was consumed by workers laboring in the fields under the fiery Andalusian sun. White gazpacho's pure color, creamy consistency, and garlicky taste are tempered by sweet green grapes. The cumin and shrimp, although not traditional, provide an intriguing and subtle flavor accent.

Makes 4 servings

1 cup/250 mL slivered blanched almonds	1 tbsp/15 mL sherry vinegar
2 cloves garlic, coarsely chopped	2 cups/500 mL ice water
½ tsp/2 mL ground cumin	16–24 skinned seedless green grapes, or 16 small balls of green melon or peeled apple
½ tsp/2 mL kosher or sea salt	
4 slices firm-textured French-style bread, crusts removed	12 small cooked shelled shrimp (optional)
½ cup/125 mL mild extra-virgin olive oil	

Put the almonds, garlic, cumin, and salt in a food processor and process until as smooth as possible. Meanwhile, soak the bread in cold water, then squeeze it to extract most of the moisture. With the motor running, gradually add the bread to the almond mixture.

Still with the motor running, pour in the oil in a thin stream, then add the vinegar, scraping down the bowl occasionally with a rubber spatula. Add 1 cup/250 mL ice water and process until smooth.

Pour the soup into a large bowl and stir in the remaining ice water. Strain the soup through a fine sieve, pressing on the solids with the back of a metal soup ladle to extract as much liquid as possible. Cover and refrigerate for several hours or overnight until well chilled.

Before serving, season with more vinegar and salt to taste if necessary. Ladle into small soup bowls and serve very cold, garnished with the grapes and shrimp. ✖

Gazpacho Andaluz
Andalusian Red Gazpacho

Although gazpacho originated in the southern lands of Andalucía, it is today one of the most universally loved soups in the world. Often called "liquid salad," it is the ultimate summer cooler, and there is absolutely nothing like it on hot, steamy days. This version comes from my mother-in-law, and it is a paradigm of fine gazpacho, using tomatoes ripened under the Andalusian sun, the finest sherry vinegar made nearby in Jerez de la Frontera, and Córdoba's superb *hojiblanca* olive oil.

Makes 6 servings

- 2½ lb/1.2 kg very ripe, flavorful tomatoes, quartered
- 1 medium green bell pepper (capsicum), seeded and coarsely chopped
- 1 pickling (kirby) cucumber, peeled, seeded, and coarsely chopped
- 1 small Vidalia onion, coarsely chopped
- 2 cloves garlic, coarsely chopped
- 1 2-inch/5 cm cube firm-textured French-style bread (no crust)

- 2 tbsp/30 mL sherry vinegar
- 2 tsp/10 mL kosher or sea salt
- 1 tsp/5 mL granulated sugar
- ½ tsp/2 mL ground cumin (optional)
- ½ cup/125 mL mild extra-virgin olive oil
- Finely chopped red and green bell peppers (capsicums) for garnish (optional)

Put half of the tomatoes, the green pepper, cucumber, onion, garlic, bread, vinegar, salt, sugar, and cumin in a food processor, and process until no large pieces remain. With the motor running, add the remaining tomatoes and process until fairly smooth. Still with the motor running, pour in the oil in a thin stream. Process until as smooth as possible.

Pass through a food mill or strain through a fine sieve, pressing on the solids with the back of a metal soup ladle to extract as much liquid as possible. Cover and refrigerate for several hours or overnight until well chilled.

Before serving, season with more vinegar and salt to taste if necessary. Ladle into small soup bowls and serve very cold, passing bowls of the red and green peppers so that guests can help themselves. ✄

Sopa Castellana Del Siglo XV

Castilian Garlic Soup

This earthy soup—among the simplest imaginable—has nourished generation upon generation of Spaniards. Traditionally made with only water, oil, garlic, and bread, it is the quintessential poor man's soup. Once peppers were introduced from America at the end of the 15th century another flavor element was added, somewhat enriching the soup but still leaving it primitive and uncomplicated—a miracle of alchemy, as one Spanish writer raves. Many cooks consider an earthenware soup tureen and bowls another essential element to the soup's flavor. A common addition is an egg per person, in which case the soup can easily be a meal.

Makes 4 servings

2   dried sweet red peppers (*ñoras*), or 1 dried New Mexico chile, stems and seeds removed

¼   cup/50 mL extra-virgin olive oil

4   cloves garlic, thinly sliced

4   ½-inch/1 cm slices good-quality country bread, cut from a small round loaf

3   oz/75 g chopped Serrano ham or prosciutto

1   tbsp/15 mL paprika, preferably Spanish smoked bittersweet

4   cups/1 L water

1   tbsp/15 mL minced parsley

½   tsp/2 mL ground cumin

    Pinch of crumbled saffron threads

    Kosher or sea salt

    Freshly ground pepper

4   eggs

Soak the dried peppers in a bowl of warm water for about 20 minutes until pliable. Scrape the flesh from the peppers and set aside.

Heat the oil over medium heat in a shallow flameproof casserole, preferably a Spanish earthenware cazuela. Add the garlic and sauté until golden on all sides. Remove the garlic with a slotted spoon and set aside. Add the bread to the casserole and fry until the slices are golden on both sides. Remove the bread and set aside.

Stir in the ham, cook for 1 minute, then sprinkle in the paprika. Pour in the water, add the dried red pepper flesh, and bring to a boil. Stir in the parsley, cumin, saffron, and salt and pepper to taste. Simmer for 30 minutes.

Preheat the oven to 450°F/230°C. Ladle soup into individual ovenproof flat-bottom bowls, preferably Spanish earthenware cazuelas. Divide the garlic and the bread slices among the bowls. Break 1 egg into a cup and slide the egg into one of the bowls. Repeat with remaining eggs. Transfer bowls to the oven and bake for about 4 minutes until the eggs are just set. ✖

Sopa De Pescado Con Pimentón

Fish Soup with Dried Red Peppers

Even though it is prepared with a minimum of ingredients, cumin and dried red peppers make this tasty soup special. Pimentón usually translates as paprika, but here it refers to the dried peppers commonly used in home cooking in southeastern Spain.

Makes 4 small servings

2 cups/500 mL fish broth or clam juice	½ Vidalia onion, thinly sliced
8 oz/225 g sea bass, grouper, or snapper fillets, skin removed	2 sprigs parsley
1 cup/250 mL water	1 bay leaf
½ cup/125 mL dry white wine	Kosher or sea salt
2 medium plum (Roma) tomatoes	3 cloves garlic, minced
1 small leek (white part only), thinly sliced	¼ tsp/1 mL ground cumin
2 dried sweet red peppers (ñoras), or 1 dried New Mexico chile, stems and seeds removed	Freshly ground pepper
	4 tsp/20 mL extra-virgin olive oil
	8–12 very small cooked shelled shrimp

Combine the broth, fish, water, wine, whole tomatoes, leek, dried peppers, onion, parsley, bay leaf, and salt to taste in a large pot. Bring to a boil. Cover and simmer for 30 minutes. Remove the fish to a board and cut into ½-inch/1 cm cubes.

Scrape the flesh from the peppers into a mortar, then mash to a paste. Add the garlic, cumin, and pepper to taste, and mash until smooth. Mash in the oil, then gently mash in the tomatoes, discarding their skins. Return the mortar mixture and the fish to the pot. Reheat before serving. Discard the bay leaf and season with salt to taste. Ladle into bowls and garnish with the shrimp. ✖

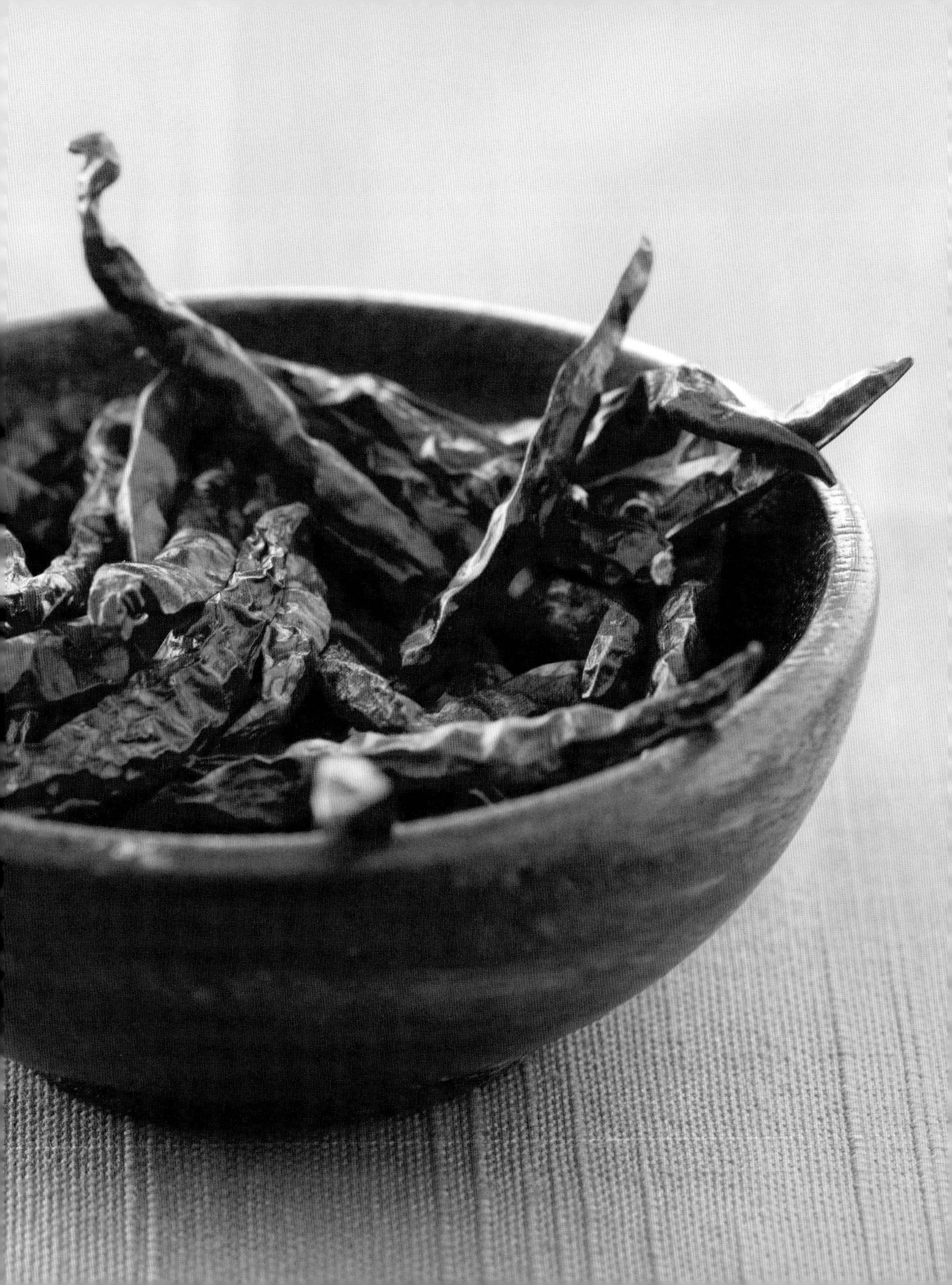

Sopa De Patatas Con Rovellones

Potato and Mushroom Soup

A soup from the stark majestic mountain range of the Maestrazgo in the region of Aragón, where the terrain is ideal for truffles and wild mushrooms. This is a lovely, well-seasoned broth slightly thickened with the potato and scattered with ham. The soup gains in flavor if left to sit for at least 30 minutes before serving.

Makes 4 servings

- 1 tbsp/15 mL extra-virgin olive oil
- 1 small Vidalia onion, finely chopped
- 2 cloves garlic, minced
- 1 small tomato, halved, seeded, and chopped
- 8 oz/225 g shitake mushrooms, brushed clean, stems trimmed, and caps finely chopped
- 1 medium (2½-inch/6 cm diameter) new potato, scrubbed and finely grated
- ⅓ cup/75 mL diced Serrano ham or prosciutto
- 2 tbsp/30 mL minced parsley
- 1½ tsp/7 mL minced fresh rosemary leaves or ¼ tsp/1 mL dried rosemary

- 1½ tsp/7 mL minced fresh thyme leaves or ¼ tsp/1 mL dried thyme
- ¼ tsp/1 mL sweet paprika, preferably Spanish smoked
- Pinch of crumbled saffron threads
- 1 bay leaf
- Kosher or sea salt
- Freshly ground pepper
- 4 cups/1 L chicken broth

Heat the oil in a large pot over medium heat and sauté the onion and garlic until softened. Add the tomato, cook for 1 minute, then add the mushrooms, potato, ham, parsley, rosemary, thyme, paprika, saffron, bay leaf, and salt and pepper to taste. Stir in the broth and bring to a boil. Cover and simmer for about 1 hour until the potatoes have disintegrated and the soup has thickened slightly. Discard the bay leaf and season with more salt and pepper to taste. Ladle into soup bowls. ✖

Caldo De El Bierzo

Vegetable Soup from El Bierzo

The tiny village of Compludo is in the fertile valley of El Bierzo in the Castilian province of León, which is famous for its fine wines. The outstanding quality of the valley's vegetables contributes to a beautifully flavored soup that's good by the cup or as a light meal.

Makes 6 servings

1   ham bone or ham hock

1   4-oz/120 g piece Serrano ham or prosciutto

½   medium Vidalia onion, finely chopped

3   cloves garlic, peeled and lightly crushed

2   bay leaves

1   sprig thyme or ¼ tsp/1 mL dried thyme

Kosher or sea salt

Freshly ground pepper

3   cups/750 mL coarsely chopped greens, such as Swiss chard or collard greens

8   very small (1½-inch/3.5 cm diameter) new potatoes, scrubbed and cut into ¾-inch/1.5 cm dice

6   tbsp/90 mL finely chopped leek (white part only)

1   cup/250 mL fresh or frozen peas

2   tbsp/30 mL minced shallots

1   tbsp/15 mL extra-virgin olive oil

½   tsp/2 mL ground cumin

½   tsp/2 mL sweet paprika, preferably Spanish smoked

Pinch of crumbled saffron threads

1   small cured chorizo sausage (about 2 oz/50 g), thinly sliced

Bring 7 cups/1.7 L water to a boil in a large pot over high heat. Add the ham bone, Serrano ham, onion, garlic, bay leaves, thyme, and salt and pepper to taste. Return to a boil. Cover and simmer for 1¼ hours.

Add the greens, potatoes, leek, peas, shallots, oil, cumin, paprika, and saffron. Simmer for 45 minutes until vegetables are very tender. Discard the ham bone, bay leaves, and thyme sprig. Add the chorizo and season with more salt and pepper to taste. Ladle into soup bowls. ✄

Sopa De Lentejas Al Estilo Madrileño
Lentil Soup Madrid-Style

Lentils have been a staple of the Western diet for millennia. Literary references to lentils appear at least as far back as the Bible in which the tale is told of Esau, who sold his birthright to his twin brother Jacob—all for a bowl of lentil soup. In Spain today, lentil soup is still common fare in most households, not only for its nutritional value, but because it makes a delicious and satisfying cold-weather meal. If using Spanish lentils, they must be soaked overnight; American lentils need not be.

Makes 4–6 servings

2¼	cups/550 mL dried lentils, preferably Spanish	4	cloves garlic, minced
1	4-oz/120 g piece salt pork or slab bacon, cut into chunks	3	tbsp/45 mL red wine vinegar
1	medium Vidalia onion, peeled	2	tsp/10 mL sweet or bittersweet paprika, preferably Spanish smoked
1	whole head garlic, loose skin removed	6	small (1½-inch/3.5 cm diameter) new potatoes, scrubbed
2	bay leaves	8	oz/225 g morcilla (Spanish blood sausage), in one piece
2	sprigs parsley		Kosher or sea salt
3	tbsp/45 mL extra-virgin olive oil		Freshly ground pepper
2	Vidalia onions, finely chopped		
2	carrots, finely chopped		

If using Spanish lentils, soak them overnight at room temperature in enough cold water to cover them. Drain well.

Put lentils in a large pot with the salt pork, whole onion, whole head of garlic, bay leaves, parsley, and about 6 cups/1.5 L water. Bring to a boil over high heat. Cover and simmer for 45 minutes.

Meanwhile, heat the oil in a skillet over medium heat and sauté the chopped onion, carrots, and minced garlic until the onion is softened. Stir in the vinegar and paprika. Add this mixture to the lentils, along with the potatoes, morcilla, and salt to taste. Bring to a boil over high heat. Cover and simmer for 45 minutes until the lentils and potatoes are tender.

Discard the whole onion, whole head of garlic, and bay leaves. Season soup with pepper and more salt to taste. Remove morcilla; cut into thin slices. Divide morcilla and potatoes among soup bowls; ladle soup into bowls. ✖

Sopa De Albondiguillas Y Alcachofas

Tiny Meatball and Artichoke Soup

The little pork meatballs studded with Serrano ham and pine nuts, and with a touch of cinnamon, make an exceptionally tasty contribution to this uncommon soup.

Makes 4 servings

- 3 tbsp/45 mL fresh breadcrumbs
- 4 cups/1 L plus 2 tbsp/30 mL chicken broth, preferably homemade
- 1 lb/500 g lean ground pork, or a mixture of ground pork and veal
- 1 egg, separated
- 2 tbsp/30 mL finely chopped pine nuts
- 2 tbsp/30 mL minced fresh mint leaves or 1 tsp/5 mL dried mint
- 1 tbsp/15 mL minced Serrano ham
- 1 tbsp/15 mL minced parsley
- 2 cloves garlic, minced

- Pinch of cinnamon
- Kosher or sea salt
- Freshly ground pepper
- 3 tbsp/45 mL extra-virgin olive oil
- ¼ medium Vidalia onion, finely chopped
- ½ tsp/2 mL sweet paprika, preferably Spanish smoked
- 4–6 cooked fresh or frozen artichoke hearts, quartered
- 1 ½-inch/1 cm slice firm-textured French-style bread, crusts removed

Soak the breadcrumbs in 2 tbsp/30 mL chicken broth in a medium bowl. Add the pork, egg yolk, pine nuts, mint, ham, parsley, garlic, cinnamon, 1¼ tsp/6 mL salt, and a grinding of pepper. Mix lightly with your hands. Shape into ¾-inch/1.5 cm meatballs.

Whisk the egg white with a fork in a separate bowl until foamy. Heat 2 tbsp/30 mL oil in a shallow flameproof casserole over medium-high heat. Dip the meatballs in the egg white to coat completely, then sauté until browned and barely cooked through. Remove to a warm platter and wipe out the casserole.

Heat the remaining oil in the casserole over medium heat, and sauté the onion until softened. Stir in the paprika, then add the remaining broth, the meatballs, and artichokes. Bring to a boil over high heat. Simmer, uncovered, for 15 minutes.

Break up the bread slice and combine in a small bowl with ¼ cup/50 mL broth from the casserole. Whisk until smooth. Stir into the soup and season with more salt to taste. Ladle into soup bowls. ✖

Crema De Cangrejos
Creamy Crayfish Soup

You might wonder why a shellfish soup is a traditional dish in a restaurant on the central plains of Spain, so far from the sea. Simply because it's made with river crabs (crayfish), and they are very much a part of local cooking. If you can find fresh crayfish, by all means use them. Otherwise a small lobster is an excellent substitute. Although from humble origins, *crema de cangrejos* can be served as part of a most refined meal.

    Purchase your lobster or crayfish alive, then have your fishmonger kill them, leaving them whole. Prepare the soup the same day. The directions for the crayfish are the same as for the lobster, except the crayfish tails are left whole and the heads and claws need not be cut up.

Makes 4 servings

1 dried sweet red pepper (*ñora*), or ½ dried New Mexico chile, stems and seeds removed	½ cup/125 mL dry white wine
1 1¼–1 ½ lb/625–750 g freshly killed lobster or 24–30 crayfish	1 leek (white part only), thinly sliced
3 tbsp/45 mL unsalted butter	1½ tsp/7 mL minced fresh thyme leaves or ¼ tsp/1 mL dried thyme
1 tbsp/15 mL extra-virgin olive oil	Pinch of crumbled saffron threads
½ medium carrot, chopped	Pinch of sweet paprika, preferably Spanish smoked
¼ medium Vidalia onion, chopped	Kosher or sea salt
1 bay leaf	Freshly ground pepper
1 small tomato, chopped	2 egg yolks
1 tbsp/15 mL minced parsley	Small cooked shelled shrimp for garnish
3 tbsp/45 mL brandy	Small fried or baked croutons for garnish
1 cup/250 mL fish broth or clam juice	

Soak the dried peppers in a bowl of warm water for about 20 minutes until pliable. Leaving the shell on and reserving as much of its liquid as possible, cut the tail from the lobster and cut crosswise into 3 slices. Open the head and transfer the green matter (tomalley) to a large mortar. Cut the head into 4 pieces. Divide each large claw into two pieces and crush lightly for easy removal of the meat. Leave the small claws whole.

Heat 1 tbsp/15 mL butter and the oil in a large pot over medium heat and sauté the carrot, onion, and bay leaf until the onion is softened. Stir in the tomato and parsley, and sauté for 3 minutes. Add the lobster pieces and sauté over high heat for 5 minutes, turning once. Standing back, add the brandy and ignite it. When the flames die down, stir in the fish broth and wine. Bring to a boil. Cover and simmer for 10 minutes.

Remove the lobster pieces to a platter. When cool enough to handle, shell the tail and large claws, cutting the meat into ½-inch/1 cm pieces. Reserve the shells and small claws. Add the head to the mortar with the tomalley and mash lightly. Return the head and tomalley to the pot, along with all of the lobster shells and small claws.

Scrape the flesh from the soaked pepper and add to the pot, along with 3¾ cups/925 mL water, the leek, thyme, saffron, paprika, and salt and pepper to taste. Bring to a boil over high heat. Cover and simmer for 45 minutes. Strain through a fine sieve and return the broth to the pot.

Whisk the egg yolks in a small bowl, then stir in some of the hot broth. Stir the egg-yolk mixture back into the pot. Stir in the remaining butter, reserved lobster meat, and shrimp. Reheat before serving but do not boil. Ladle into soup bowls and garnish with croutons. ✖

Rice and Pasta

Arroz A La Zamorana

Rice with Pork and Paprika, Zamora-Style

You wouldn't think that a rice dish would be a specialty so far from rice country, and yet *arroz a la zamorana*, prepared in an earthenware casserole instead of a paella pan, and relying on pork instead of seafood, has a long tradition. It is said that in times past the famous muleteers of León brought rice to landlocked northern Zamora province from their trips to the eastern Valencian coast, where it became an integral part of traditional cooking. Obviously the rice dishes in this region do not feature products of the sea, nor a wide range of vegetables, but a goodly amount of paprika, a variety of pork products, and Zamora's famous chickpeas create exceptional flavor.

Makes 4 servings

8	cloves garlic, minced
3	tbsp/45 mL minced parsley
	Pinch of crumbled saffron threads
	Kosher or sea salt
1	pig's foot, split
1	pig's ear
1	bay leaf
	Freshly ground pepper
2	medium turnips (about 8 oz/225 g), peeled and cut into ¼-inch/5 mm slices
2	tbsp/30 mL extra-virgin olive oil
4	oz/120 g boneless pork loin, cut into ½-inch/1 cm pieces
1	medium Vidalia onion, finely chopped
1	medium green bell pepper (capsicum), seeded and finely chopped

1½	tsp/7 mL minced fresh thyme leaves or ¼ tsp/1 mL dried thyme
¼	tsp/1 mL dried oregano
1	small tomato, finely chopped
2	tbsp/30 mL diced Serrano ham or prosciutto
1¾	cups/425 mL Valencian short-grain or Arborio rice
1½	tsp/7 mL paprika, preferably Spanish smoked bittersweet
⅔	cup/150 mL drained cooked chickpeas

Mash 2 cloves garlic, 1 tbsp/15 mL parsley, the saffron, and a pinch of salt to a paste in a mortar, or process in a mini food processor until finely minced. Set aside.

Combine 6 cups/1.5 L water, the pig's foot, pig's ear, bay leaf, and salt and pepper to taste in a large deep pot. Bring to a boil over high heat. Cover and simmer for 1¼ hours. Add the turnips, and simmer for 15 minutes until turnips are tender. Remove pig's foot and ear, and turnips from the pot. When cool enough to handle, remove the bones from the foot and ear, and finely chop the meat. Measure the cooking liquid. You should have 3½ cups/875 mL; if there's too much, boil the liquid over high heat to reduce it.

Preheat the oven to 400°F/200°C. In a shallow 15-inch/38 cm diameter flameproof casserole, preferably a Spanish earthenware cazuela, heat the oil over medium heat and sauté the pork loin until it loses its color. Add the onion, green pepper, remaining garlic and parsley, the thyme, oregano, and black pepper to taste, and sauté until the onion is softened. Stir in the tomato, ham, and reserved meat from pig's foot and ear, and sauté for 2 minutes. Stir in the rice, and sauté until it has absorbed some of the oil. Stir in the paprika, then add the reserved broth and bring to a boil over high heat. Season generously with salt to taste. Boil for 10 minutes until the rice is no longer soupy but some liquid remains. Stir in the garlic-parsley paste, turnips, and chickpeas.

Transfer the casserole to the oven. Bake, uncovered, until the rice is almost al dente, about 13 minutes in a gas oven, 15–20 minutes in an electric one. Remove the pan from the oven, cover with foil, and let stand in a warm place for 5–10 minutes until the rice is cooked to taste. Serve straight from the dish. ◉

Paella De Cerdo, Pollo Y Salchicha Con Costra

Egg-Crusted Pork, Chicken, and Sausage Paella

What really makes this paella exceptional is its unusual and delicious egg crust. It is one of the mind-boggling 148 kinds of paella made daily at Dársena, a restaurant in the port area of the city of Alicante.

Makes 4 servings

3 cups/750 mL chicken broth

½ cup/125 mL dry white wine

Pinch of crumbled saffron threads

⅓ cup/75 mL extra-virgin olive oil

1 boneless, skinless chicken thigh, cut into ½-inch/1 cm pieces

4 oz/120 g boneless pork loin, cut into ½-inch/1 cm pieces

4 oz/120 g sweet cured chorizo, cut diagonally into ½-inch/1 cm slices

1 red bell pepper (capsicum), seeded and finely chopped

1 small Vidalia onion, finely chopped

3 cloves garlic, minced

1¾ cups/425 mL Valencian short-grain or Arborio rice

⅔ cup/150 mL drained cooked chickpeas

1 small tomato, finely chopped

1 tbsp/15 mL minced parsley

½ tsp/2 mL paprika, preferably Spanish smoked bittersweet

Kosher or sea salt

2 tbsp/30 mL mayonnaise

4 eggs

Preheat the oven to 400°F/200°C if using a gas oven, 450°F/230°C if using an electric one. Heat the broth, wine, and saffron in a medium saucepan over medium heat, then keep hot over low heat.

In a paella pan that measures 13 inches/33 cm across the top, or in a shallow 13-inch/33 cm diameter flameproof casserole, heat the oil over medium-high heat and sauté the chicken, pork, and chorizo until golden. Transfer to a plate.

Add the red pepper, onion, and garlic to the paella pan and sauté over medium heat until softened. Return the chicken, pork, and chorizo to the pan and sauté for 1 minute. Stir in the rice, chickpeas, tomato, parsley, and paprika. Pour in the hot broth and bring to a boil over high heat. Season generously with salt to taste. Boil for about 5 minutes, stirring occasionally, until the rice is no longer soupy but sufficient liquid remains to continue cooking the rice.

Transfer the pan to the oven. Bake, uncovered, until the rice is almost al dente, 10–12 minutes in a gas oven, 15–20 in an electric one. Remove from the oven and increase the oven temperature to 550°F/285°C.

Put the mayonnaise in a medium bowl and whisk in the eggs one at a time. Pour mayonnaise mixture evenly over the rice and return the pan to the oven for 5 minutes until the egg mixture is lightly brown. Let stand, uncovered, for 5 minutes before serving straight from the pan. ◉

Andrajos De Úbeda

Dried Cod, Shrimp, and Pasta Stew

Start preparing this noodle dish two to three days in advance. *Andrajos* are literally rags, and refer to the strips of pasta that are part of this dish and provide the ideal contrast to the somewhat strong taste of salt cod. Somewhere between a soup and a stew, this is one of the few uniquely Spanish pasta preparations.

Makes 4 servings

For homemade pasta:

- 1   cup/250 mL all-purpose flour
- ¼   tsp/1 mL table salt
- ½   cup/125 mL (approx.) cold water

For stew:

- 4   oz/120 g skinless, boneless salt cod, soaked in cold water to cover in the refrigerator for 2–3 days (change the water once or twice daily)
- 3   tbsp/45 mL extra-virgin olive oil
- 8   fresh or frozen artichoke hearts, quartered
- 1   green bell pepper (capsicum), seeded and finely diced
- 1   medium Vidalia onion, finely chopped
- 3   medium tomatoes, finely chopped
- 2   tsp/10 mL granulated sugar
- ¼   tsp/1 mL sweet paprika, preferably Spanish smoked

- ¼   tsp/1 mL hot paprika, preferably Spanish smoked

    Kosher or sea salt

- 3   cups/750 mL fish broth
- 2   large cloves garlic, minced
- 2   minced fresh mint leaves or a pinch of dried mint

    Pinch of crumbled saffron threads

- ¼   cup/50 mL dry white wine
- 10   medium shrimp, shelled, deveined, and cut into thirds

    Freshly ground pepper

- 1   tbsp/15 mL minced parsley

To prepare the homemade pasta, combine the flour and salt in a medium bowl. Stir in enough water so that the dough holds together (you may not need all of the water). Turn the dough out onto a lightly floured work surface, and knead to form a smooth elastic dough, adding a little more flour if necessary. Roll out the dough very thinly and cut into twelve 2½-inch/6 cm rounds. Cut each round into quarters and set aside.

To prepare the stew, drain the cod and dry on paper towels. Heat 1 tbsp/15 mL oil in a medium skillet over medium heat and sauté the cod for 10 minutes until tender. Remove the cod from the skillet. Let cool, then flake finely and set aside. Wipe out the skillet.

Heat the remaining oil in the skillet over medium heat and sauté the artichokes, green pepper, and onion until the green pepper and onion are softened. Add the tomatoes, sugar, sweet and hot paprikas, and salt to taste, and sauté for 10 minutes. Stir in the broth and bring to a boil over high heat. Simmer, uncovered, for 30 minutes.

Mash the garlic, mint, and saffron to a paste in a mortar or process in a mini food processor until finely minced. Stir in the wine until well combined, then add the mortar mixture to the skillet and cook for 10 minutes. Add the cod and shrimp to the skillet and simmer for 5 minutes. Scatter in the pasta pieces and continue cooking until the pasta is al dente, about 15–20 minutes. The mixture should be soupy so add more broth or water if necessary. Season with pepper to taste. Ladle into soup bowls, preferably flat-bottomed earthenware bowls, and serve sprinkled with parsley. ◉

Arroz Con Calamares, Coliflor Y Alcachofas

Squid, Cauliflower, and Artichoke Paella

Artichoke, cauliflower, and squid blend superbly in this paella. Remember that in Valencia, where rice is eaten daily, almost any additional ingredient is welcomed, and this paella showcases several exceptional possibilities.

Makes 4–6 servings

6 cloves garlic, minced	2 cups/500 mL small cauliflower florets (no stems)
2 tbsp/30 mL minced parsley	1 medium tomato, finely chopped
¼ tsp/1 mL crumbled saffron threads	2½ cups/625 mL Valencian short-grain or Arborio rice
5 cups/1.2 L clam juice or fish broth	¼ cup/50 mL fresh or frozen peas
7 tbsp/105 mL extra-virgin olive oil	½ tsp/2 mL sweet paprika, preferably Spanish smoked
8 oz/225 g cleaned squid, cut into ½-inch/1 cm pieces	Freshly ground pepper
2 green bell peppers (capsicums), seeded and finely chopped	Kosher or sea salt
1 medium Vidalia onion, finely chopped	Strips of pimiento for garnish
4 fresh or frozen artichoke hearts, quartered	

Preheat the oven to 400°F/200°C if using a gas oven, 450°F/230°C if using an electric one.

Mash garlic, parsley, and saffron to a smooth paste in a mortar, or process in a mini food processor until finely minced. Set aside. Heat the clam juice in a medium saucepan over medium heat, then keep hot over low heat.

In a paella pan that measures 17–18 inches/42–45 cm across the top, heat the oil over medium-high heat, positioning pan over two burners if necessary. Sauté the squid, green peppers, and onion, until peppers and onion are softened. Add the artichokes, cauliflower, and tomato, and sauté for 3 minutes. Stir in the rice, peas, paprika, and pepper to taste. Pour in the hot clam juice, then bring to a boil over high heat. Stir in mortar mixture and salt to taste. Boil for about 5 minutes, stirring occasionally, until the rice is no longer soupy but sufficient liquid remains to continue cooking the rice.

Arrange strips of pimiento over the rice. Transfer the pan to the oven. Bake, uncovered, until the rice is almost al dente, 10–12 minutes in a gas oven, 15–20 in an electric one. Remove the pan from the oven, cover with foil, and let stand in a warm place for 5–10 minutes until the rice is cooked to taste. Serve straight from the pan. ◉

Andrajos Con Chorizo

Chorizo, Tomato, and Pasta Stew

Although the tomato and pasta temper the spiciness of the chorizo, this stew, typical of Jaén, is still a hearty dish. In this Andalusian province, olive trees climb in dizzying rows up and down the hillsides, and are the very heart and soul of the place. In fact, Jaén alone produces fully 20 per cent of the world's olive oil.

Makes 4 servings

3 tbsp/45 mL extra-virgin olive oil	1 tsp/5 mL hot paprika, preferably Spanish smoked
1 medium Vidalia onion, finely chopped	1 bay leaf
4 cloves garlic, minced	1¼ cups/300 mL chicken broth
¾ lb/400 g sweet chorizo, skinned and cut into ½-inch/1 cm pieces	½ cup/125 mL dry white wine
5 medium plum (Roma) tomatoes, chopped	Kosher or sea salt
⅓ cup/75 mL tomato sauce	Freshly ground pepper
1 tbsp/15 mL minced fresh thyme leaves or ½ tsp/2 mL dried thyme	Homemade pasta (p. 50)

Heat the oil in a large shallow flameproof casserole over medium heat and sauté the onion and garlic until the onion is softened. Add the chorizo and sauté for 2 minutes. Stir in the tomatoes, tomato sauce, thyme, paprika, and bay leaf, and cook for 5 minutes. Add the broth, wine, and salt and pepper to taste, and bring to a boil over high heat. Simmer, uncovered, for 30 minutes.

Add the pasta, submerging it in the broth, and cook, uncovered, for about 15–20 minutes until pasta is al dente, stirring occasionally, and adding a little more broth if necessary (the stew should be slightly soupy). Discard the bay leaf and ladle the stew into shallow soup bowls, preferably flat-bottomed earthenware bowls. ◉

Paella De Verduras

Mixed Vegetable Paella

On the reed-lined banks of one of the many canals that run through the Valencian town of El Palmar, each and every restaurant is dedicated to paella. This version is made with the vegetables that grow in abundance in Valencia, a region often called the "Garden of Spain." It's cooked over orange tree wood (Valencia's other claim to fame is its orange groves) which creates the *socarrat*—a crisp crust of rice that sticks to the bottom of the paella pan.

Makes 4 servings

1½ cups/375 mL vegetable broth	8 baby carrots (about 3 oz/75 g), finely chopped
Pinch of crumbled saffron threads	8 shitake mushrooms, brushed clean, stems trimmed, and caps coarsely chopped
Kosher or sea salt	
3 tbsp/45 mL extra-virgin olive oil	1 bunch scallions, trimmed and finely chopped
2 medium red bell peppers (capsicums), seeded and cut into ½-inch/1 cm pieces	2 cloves garlic, minced
	½ cup/125 mL chopped tomatoes
1 medium zucchini (about 6 oz/175 g), cut into ½-inch/1 cm pieces	1 tsp/5 mL sweet paprika, preferably Spanish smoked
4 oz/120 g snap peas or snow peas, strings removed	1¼ cups/300 mL Valencian short-grain or Arborio rice
4 oz/120 g green beans, preferably broad flat beans, trimmed and cut into 1-inch/2.5 cm pieces	

Preheat the oven to 400°F/200°C if using a gas oven, 450°F/230°C if using an electric one.

Heat the vegetable broth, 1 cup/250 mL water, the saffron, and a pinch of salt in a medium saucepan over medium heat, then keep hot over low heat.

In a paella pan that measures 13 inches/32 cm across the top, heat the oil over high heat. Add the red peppers, zucchini, peas, beans, carrots, mushrooms, and scallions, and sauté for about 10 minutes until vegetables start to soften. Add the garlic and sauté for 2 minutes. Add the tomatoes and paprika and cook for 1 minute. Stir in the rice. Pour in the hot broth, then bring to a boil over high heat. Season generously with salt to taste. Boil for about 5 minutes, stirring occasionally, until the rice is no longer soupy but sufficient liquid remains to continue cooking the rice.

Transfer the pan to the oven. Bake, uncovered, until the rice is almost al dente, 10–12 minutes in a gas oven, 15–20 in an electric one. Remove the pan from the oven, cover with foil, and let stand in a warm place for 5–10 minutes until the rice is cooked to taste.

To make the *socarrat*, uncover the pan, place over burner, and cook over medium-high heat, without stirring, for about 2 minutes until a crust of rice forms on the bottom of the pan (be careful not to let it burn). Serve straight from the pan. ◉

Tallarines De Quesada

Pasta, Rabbit, and Green Bean Stew

This version of the pasta dish called *andrajos*, from the small village of Quesada in southeastern Spain, is locally called *tallarines*. The blend of dried red pepper (*ñora*), garlic, and peppercorns is outstanding. Have your butcher chop up the rabbit for you.

Makes 4 servings

- 1 3-lb/1.5 kg rabbit, cut into 1½–2-inch/ 3.5–5 cm pieces, bony leg tips removed
   Kosher or sea salt
- 2 tbsp/30 mL extra-virgin olive oil
- 2 dried sweet red peppers (*ñoras*) or 1 dried New Mexico chile, stems and seeds removed
- 2 cloves garlic, minced
- 12 peppercorns
   Kosher or sea salt
- 1½ cups/375 mL plus 2 tsp/10 mL chicken broth
- 1 red bell pepper (capsicum), seeded and finely chopped

- 1 small Vidalia onion, finely chopped
- 1½ tsp/7 mL minced fresh thyme leaves or ¼ tsp/1 mL dried thyme
- 1 bay leaf
- 1 medium tomato, finely chopped
- 8 oz/225 g green beans, preferably broad flat beans, trimmed and cut into 1-inch/2.5 cm pieces
   Homemade pasta (p. 50) or 8 fresh lasagna sheets, torn in half crosswise

Sprinkle the rabbit with salt and set aside. Heat the oil in a large shallow flameproof casserole over medium heat and slowly sauté the dried peppers, turning occasionally, until slightly softened. Transfer to a mortar, leaving the oil in the casserole. Add the garlic, peppercorns, and ½ tsp/2 mL salt to the mortar and mash as finely as possible. Add 2 tsp/10 mL chicken broth and continue mashing to a paste, adding a little more broth if necessary. Set aside.

Reheat the oil in the casserole over medium heat and add the red pepper, onion, thyme, and bay leaf. Sauté until the vegetables are softened. Stir in the tomato, and sauté for 5 minutes. Add the rabbit, and sauté, turning once, until it turns white but doesn't brown.

Stir in the green beans, remaining chicken broth, and salt to taste and bring to a boil over high heat. Cover and simmer 20 minutes. Add the pasta, submerging it in the broth, and cook, uncovered, for about 20 minutes until pasta is al dente, stirring occasionally, and adding a little more broth if necessary (the stew should be slightly soupy). Discard the bay leaf and ladle the stew into shallow soup bowls, preferably flat-bottomed earthenware bowls. ◉

Paella De Mejillones

Mussel Paella

This simple paella relies almost entirely on mussels for its superb flavor. The shellfish are typically little more than decorative notes to a seafood paella, but here mussels are the star attraction. In Valencia, rice was—and continues to be—a staple that was eaten every day, and there was nothing cheaper than a paella made with mussels.

This paella shows once more how simple, fresh ingredients can produce excellent results. If you use cultivated mussels, the overnight soaking is probably not necessary since they will not be sandy. And if the mussels are not cultivated, you will probably need fewer because they tend to be larger. The amount of mussels may seem excessive, but keep in mind that about half are chopped and blended into the rice, while the rest will garnish the paella and be eaten from the shell.

Makes 6–8 servings

6	lb/3 kg mussels, preferably small cultivated mussels, soaked in cold salted water for several hours or overnight
⅔	cup/150 mL dry white wine
5¼	cups/1.3 L (approx.) clam juice or fish broth
¼	cup/50 mL freshly squeezed lemon juice
1	tbsp/15 mL minced fresh rosemary leaves or ½ tsp/2 mL dried rosemary
1	tbsp/15 mL minced fresh thyme leaves or ½ tsp/2 mL dried thyme
¼	tsp/1 mL crumbled saffron threads
7	tbsp/105 mL extra-virgin olive oil
1	medium Vidalia onion, finely chopped
8	cloves garlic, minced

¼	cup/50 mL minced parsley
2	tbsp/30 mL minced shallots
4	pimientos
3	cups/750 mL Valencian short-grain or Arborio rice
	Kosher or sea salt
2	tsp/10 mL paprika, preferably Spanish smoked bittersweet

Put aside 6–10 mussels per portion, depending on size. Pour the wine into a large skillet, add the remaining mussels, cover, and bring to a boil. Cook over high heat, removing the mussels to a plate as they open and reserving the cooking liquid in the skillet. Remove the mussel meat from the shells, discarding any mussels that haven't opened. Chop the mussel meat coarsely and set aside.

Measure the broth that remains in the skillet and add enough clam juice to measure 6 cups/1.5 L. Combine the clam juice mixture with the lemon juice, rosemary, thyme, and saffron in a medium saucepan. Heat over medium heat, then keep hot over low heat. Preheat the oven to 400°F/200°C if using a gas oven, 450°F/230°C if using an electric one.

In a paella pan that measures 17–18 inches/42–45 cm across the top, heat the oil over medium-high heat, positioning pan over two burners if necessary. Add the onion, garlic, parsley, and shallots, and sauté until onion and shallots have softened. Chop 2 pimientos and add to the pan, along with the chopped mussel meat. Sauté for 1 minute. Stir in the rice. Pour in the hot clam juice mixture, then bring to a boil over high heat. Season generously with salt to taste. Boil for about 5 minutes, stirring occasionally, until the rice is no longer soupy but sufficient liquid remains to continue cooking the rice.

Slice the remaining pimientos and arrange attractively over the rice, along with the reserved mussels, placing the mussels hinge side down. Transfer the pan to the oven. Bake, uncovered, until the rice is almost al dente, 10–12 minutes in a gas oven, 15–20 in an electric one. Remove the pan from the oven, cover with foil, and let stand in a warm place for 5–10 minutes until the rice is cooked to taste. Discard any mussels that haven't opened, and serve the paella straight from the pan. ◉

Paella A La Valenciana

Seafood and Meat Paella

The most popular paella outside of Spain combines fish and meats in one dish, although, in paella's homeland, such a mixture of ingredients comes close to heresy. Nevertheless, I must admit it is extremely tasty and appealing, and most colorful. Paella has no set ingredients—except rice and olive oil—and can be varied at will.

Makes 6–8 servings

½ small roasting chicken or 1 small rabbit

8 oz/225 g cleaned squid, bodies cut crosswise into ½-inch/1 cm slices and tentacles halved

8 oz/225 g monkfish or other firm-fleshed fish, skin removed, and cut in ½-inch/1 cm pieces

12–16 extra-large shrimp, in their shells

4 oz/120 g boneless pork loin, cut in ½-inch/1 cm pieces

Kosher or sea salt

6 cups/1.5 L clam juice, fish broth, or chicken broth

¼ tsp/1 mL crumbled saffron threads

½ cup/125 mL extra-virgin olive oil

4 oz/125 g cured chorizo, thinly sliced

1 medium Vidalia onion, finely chopped

1 green bell pepper (capsicum), seeded and finely chopped

6 cloves garlic, minced

1 medium tomato, finely chopped

2 tsp/10 mL sweet paprika, preferably Spanish smoked

3 cups/750 mL Valencian short-grain or Arborio rice

½ cup/125 mL fresh or frozen peas

2 tbsp/30 mL minced parsley

24–28 Manila clams or cockles, or 12–16 small littleneck clams, or 18 very small mussels

Lemon wedges and strips of pimiento for garnish

Chop off the bony ends of the chicken's leg. With sturdy kitchen shears, cut chicken into 1½-inch/3.5 cm pieces. Sprinkle the chicken, squid, monkfish, shrimp in their shells, and pork evenly with salt, and set aside.

Preheat the oven to 400°F/200°C if using a gas oven, 450°F/230°C if using an electric one. Heat the clam juice and saffron in a medium saucepan over medium heat, then keep hot over low heat.

In a paella pan that measures 17–18 inches/42–45 cm across the top, heat 6 tbsp/90 mL oil over high heat, positioning pan over two burners if necessary. Add shrimp in their shells and sauté briefly until just pink but not cooked through. Remove shrimp to a large plate. Sauté the chicken until brown but not fully cooked. Remove to the plate with the shrimp. Sauté the pork, monkfish, and chorizo for 1–2 minutes, then remove to a separate plate. Sauté the squid for 1 minute, then remove to the plate with the pork.

Heat the remaining oil in the pan over medium heat and sauté the onion, green pepper, and garlic until onion and pepper are slightly softened. Stir in the tomato and paprika and cook for 1 minute. Stir in the rice. Pour in the hot clam juice, then bring to a boil over high heat. Season generously with salt to taste. Boil for 3 minutes, stirring occasionally. Stir in the pork, monkfish, chorizo, squid, peas, and parsley and boil for about 2 minutes until the rice is no longer soupy but sufficient liquid remains to continue cooking the rice.

Arrange the chicken, shrimp, and clams over the rice, placing clams hinge side down. Transfer the pan to the oven. Bake, uncovered, until the rice is almost al dente, 10–12 minutes in a gas oven, 15–20 in an electric one. Remove the pan from the oven, cover with foil, and let stand in a warm place for 5–10 minutes until the rice is cooked to taste. Discard any clams that haven't opened. Garnish with lemon wedges and pimiento strips, and serve straight from the pan. ◉

PESCADOS Y MARISCOS

Fish and Seafood

Pulpo Encebollado A La Gallega

Octopus with Paprika in Simmered Onions

Any fish dish in Galicia described as *a la gallega* is prepared in a simple olive oil and paprika sauce. Octopus in particular is enormously popular cooked this way, and is served in just about every tapas bar, and at country festivals where it's boiled in steaming metal cauldrons. It is typically presented on small wooden dishes accompanied by Galician potatoes, drizzled with oil, and sprinkled with Spanish paprika. The unusual ritual of dunking the octopus several times in boiling water tenderizes it and gives it shape.

Makes 4 servings

- 2 octopus (1 lb/500 g each), cleaned
- 2 tbsp/30 mL extra-virgin olive oil
- 2 medium Vidalia onions, finely chopped
- 4 cloves garlic, thinly sliced
- 1½ tsp/7 mL minced fresh thyme leaves or ¼ tsp/1 mL dried thyme
- 1 bay leaf
- ¼ cup/50 mL dry white wine

- 1 tbsp/15 mL sweet paprika, preferably Spanish smoked
- Kosher or sea salt
- 1 medium potato, cooked, peeled, and cut into ½-inch/1 cm pieces
- Hot paprika, preferably Spanish smoked, for garnish

Bring a large pot of water to a boil. Dunk the octopus in the boiling water for a few seconds. Remove and repeat twice, leaving the octopus out of the water for about 1 minute between dunkings. Return the octopus to the pot. Cover and simmer for 1 hour. Drain well.

When cool enough to handle, snip off the ends of the tentacles with kitchen shears. Discard the sac-like mouths, then cut the octopus into 1-inch/2.5 cm pieces.

Heat the oil in a large saucepan over medium heat and sauté the onion, garlic, thyme, and bay leaf for 2–3 minutes. Reduce the heat to low. Cover and simmer gently for 20 minutes until the onion is very soft but not brown. Stir in the octopus, wine, sweet paprika, and salt to taste. Increase the heat to medium. Cover and cook for 10 minutes. Stir in the potato. Spoon into a shallow serving dish, and serve sprinkled with the hot paprika. ◎

Merluza A La Vasca

Hake Steaks with Clams in Wine and Parsley Sauce

This is one of the great dishes of Spain and, as is usually the case with Spanish cooking, simplicity itself. There are many variations on this dish, like the additions of peas and asparagus, but here it is in its purest—and, I think, its best—form.

Makes 4 servings

½ cup/125 mL fish broth or clam juice

½ cup/125 mL dry white wine

2 lb/1 kg hake or scrod steaks, about 1 inch/2.5 cm thick

Kosher or sea salt

6 tbsp/90 mL extra-virgin olive oil

6 cloves garlic, minced

2 1-inch/2.5 cm pieces dried hot red chile, seeded

1 tbsp/15 mL all-purpose flour

¼ cup/50 mL minced parsley

24–28 Manila clams or cockles, or 12–16 very small littlenecks, soaked in cold salted water for several hours or overnight

Boil the fish broth and wine in a small saucepan until the liquid measures ½ cup/125 mL. Set aside. Sprinkle the fish on both sides with salt and let stand at room temperature for 15 minutes.

In a shallow flameproof casserole, preferably a Spanish earthenware cazuela, or in a large skillet, heat the oil, garlic, and chile over medium heat until the garlic is pale golden. Add the fish, sprinkle with the flour and 2 tbsp/30 mL parsley, and cook for 1 minute. Add the clams, then gradually pour in the broth and cook for 2 minutes, gently shaking the casserole all the time.

Carefully turn the fish and cook for about 10 minutes, continuing to gently shake the casserole often, until the clams open and the fish flakes easily with a fork. Divide the fish among 4 dinner plates, spooning the clams and sauce around each portion, discarding any clams that don't open. Serve sprinkled with the remaining parsley. ◎

Pescado A La Parrilla Con Salsa De Anchoa

Grilled Fish with Anchovy-Caper Sauce

This anchovy sauce adds a spark to everything you pair it with—salads, boiled potatoes, and especially plain grilled fish. Its assertive taste is ideal with many foods that are mild in flavor. The sauce will keep in the refrigerator for a week or two.

Makes 4 servings

2   lb/1 kg monkfish, turbot, or swordfish steaks, about 1 inch/2.5 cm thick, cut into 4 pieces

Kosher or sea salt

For sauce:

2   tbsp/30 mL minced shallots

2   tbsp/30 mL minced parsley

2   tbsp/30 mL drained capers

4   large anchovy fillets, chopped

2   cloves garlic, minced

4   tsp/20 mL minced Vidalia onion

1½ tsp/7 mL minced fresh thyme leaves or ¼ tsp/1 mL dried thyme

¼   tsp/1 mL dried oregano

¼   tsp/1 mL ground cumin

¼   tsp/1 mL hot paprika, preferably Spanish smoked

2   tbsp/30 mL extra-virgin olive oil

1½ tbsp/22 mL red wine vinegar

Kosher or sea salt

Freshly ground pepper

Sprinkle fish with salt and let stand at room temperature while you prepare the sauce.

To prepare the sauce, mash the shallots, parsley, capers, anchovies, garlic, onion, thyme, oregano, cumin, and paprika to a paste in a mortar. Stir in the oil, vinegar, and salt and pepper to taste.

Grease a ridged grill pan and heat over high heat until very hot. Grill the fish for 8–10 minutes, turning once, until just cooked. Serve drizzled with the anchovy-caper sauce. ◎

Suquet De Pescado Con Alioli

Fish Stew with Alioli

In my view, anything served with alioli tastes extraordinary, and this Catalan fish stew, popular with fishermen and their families in northeastern Spain, is no exception. If you don't wish to make your own alioli (although it couldn't be easier to do) and cannot find ready made, improvise by combining ¾ cup/175 mL mayonnaise with 4 minced cloves of garlic, and 2 tsp/10 mL each lemon juice and extra-virgin olive oil. Serve the stew with a green salad.

Makes 4 servings

- 1 lb/500 g turbot, halibut, or other firm-fleshed fish, about 1 inch/2.5 cm thick, cut into 4 pieces
- 8 oz/225 g monkfish, about 1 inch/2.5 cm thick, cut into 4 pieces
- Kosher or sea salt
- 3 tbsp/45 mL extra-virgin olive oil
- 6 cloves garlic, minced
- 2 large plum (Roma) tomatoes, chopped
- 3 tbsp/45 mL minced parsley
- 1½ tsp/7 mL minced fresh thyme leaves or ¼ tsp/1 mL dried thyme
- 1 bay leaf
- 1½ cups/375 mL fish broth

- 6 tbsp/90 mL dry white wine
- ½ tsp/2 mL sweet paprika, preferably Spanish smoked
- ¼ tsp/1 mL crumbled saffron threads

For alioli:
- 10 cloves garlic, peeled and lightly crushed
- 1 tsp/5 mL kosher or sea salt
- 1 egg
- 1 tbsp/15 mL freshly squeezed lemon juice
- 1 cup/250 mL extra-virgin olive oil

Sprinkle the turbot and the monkfish with salt. Heat the oil in a shallow flameproof casserole over medium heat, and sauté the garlic until it begins to color. Add the tomatoes, 2 tbsp/30 mL parsley, the thyme, and bay leaf, and sauté for 2 minutes. Add the fish broth and wine, and bring to a boil over high heat. Boil for 10 minutes. Add the fish, sprinkle with the paprika and saffron, and simmer for 10 minutes until the fish flakes easily with a fork.

To prepare the alioli, process the garlic and salt in a food processor until finely minced. Add the egg and lemon juice, and process until pale. With the motor running, gradually pour in the oil and process until thick and creamy.

Remove the fish to a serving platter, sprinkle with the remaining parsley, and serve with the alioli on the side. ◎

Atún Frito Con Miel

Honey-Coated Fried Tuna

This recipe, with its Moorish sweet and savory overtones, combines fresh tuna with honey for a traditional preparation that nonetheless appears thoroughly modern. Cut the fish into 1-inch/2.5 cm cubes instead of steaks for a wonderful tapa.

Makes 4 servings

2 lb/1 kg tuna steaks, ¾–1 inch/1.5–2.5 cm thick	Pinch of crumbled saffron threads
Kosher or sea salt	Olive oil for frying
2 eggs	Liquid honey
½ tsp/2 mL ground cumin	All-purpose flour for dusting
½ tsp/2 mL dried parsley flakes	

Sprinkle the tuna on both sides with salt and let stand for 10 minutes. Beat together the eggs, cumin, parsley, and saffron in a shallow dish.

Pour oil into a large skillet to a depth of ⅛ inch/3 mm and heat over medium-high heat. Spread each side of the tuna steaks lightly with honey. Dust the steaks with flour, then coat on both sides with the egg mixture. Arrange steaks in a single layer in the skillet and cook over medium-high heat for 8–10 minutes, turning once, until the coating is golden and the tuna cooked to taste. Remove to a serving platter. ◎

Rodaballo Con Hongos

Sautéed Turbot with Mushrooms, Garlic, and Scallions

Mushrooms complement this simple yet elegant fish dish, which can be prepared in minutes.

Makes 4 servings

4 turbot or halibut steaks, about 1 inch/2.5 cm thick

Kosher or sea salt

6 tbsp/90 mL extra-virgin olive oil

⅓ cup/75 mL unsalted butter

4 cloves garlic, minced

2 tbsp/30 mL minced scallion or leek (white part only)

1 lb/500 g cremini, oyster, or shitake mushrooms, brushed clean, stems trimmed, and caps thinly sliced

1 tbsp/15 mL freshly squeezed lemon juice

1 tbsp/15 mL dry (*fino*) sherry

¼ tsp/1 mL sweet paprika, preferably Spanish smoked

2 tbsp/30 mL minced parsley

Sprinkle the fish with salt and let stand for 10 minutes. Heat the oil, butter, garlic, and scallion (or leek) in a large skillet over medium heat until the garlic just begins to sizzle. Add the mushrooms, lemon juice, sherry, paprika, and salt to taste, and sauté, adding more oil if necessary, until the mushrooms have softened, 5–7 minutes.

Meanwhile, grease a ridged grill pan and heat over high heat until very hot. Grill the fish for about 8 minutes, turning once, until just cooked. Serve topped with the mushroom mixture and sprinkled with parsley. ◎

Atún Mechado Con Cebolla Y Jerez

Baked Fresh Tuna in Sherry Sauce

This simple fish preparation has the distinctive taste of southern Spanish town of Sanlúcar de Barrameda, because of the local dry *manzanilla* sherry in which the fish simmers. Tuna is particularly delicious here in western Andalucía. It is caught in the Atlantic off the coast of Cádiz province each spring when the tuna migrate from colder waters to the Mediterranean in search of spawning grounds. At that time of year the fish still have a layer of prized winter fat, attracting Japanese buyers seeking the best of the best.

Makes 6–8 appetizer servings

- 2 1-lb/500 g pieces tuna, about 3 inches/ 8 cm thick, cut from the tail
-    Kosher or sea salt
- 2 tbsp/30 mL coarsely ground pepper
- 1 medium Vidalia onion, thinly sliced
- 4 cloves garlic, peeled and lightly crushed
- 2 bay leaves
- 1 cup/250 mL very dry sherry, such as *manzanilla*
- ½ cup/125 mL extra-virgin olive oil

Preheat the oven to 300°F/150°C. Put the tuna in a roasting pan, sprinkle with salt, and, with the heel of your hand, press the ground pepper over each piece to form a crust. Scatter the onion, garlic, and bay leaves around the fish. Pour in the sherry and oil, and sprinkle the vegetables with salt.

Bake for 45 minutes or until a meat thermometer inserted into thickest part of the fish registers 140–145°F/60–63°C. Remove the tuna to a board and let cool.

Pour the contents of the roasting pan into a medium saucepan and simmer, uncovered, for about 15 minutes until the onion has softened and the sauce is slightly reduced. Discard the bay leaves.

Pour the sauce into a food processor and pulse briefly until almost smooth (the sauce should still contain small chunks). Pour the sauce into a serving bowl. Cut the tuna crosswise into ¼-inch/ 5 mm slices and arrange on a serving platter. Serve with the sauce. ◉

Atún Fresco Con Verduras Asadas

Pickled Fresh Tuna with Roasted Vegetables

Escabeche, once a means of preserving fish, is one of Spain's great contributions to gastronomy. This version made with fresh tuna is outstanding. Use either dark tuna or white bonito—both readily available today thanks to the popularity of sushi.

Makes 4–6 servings

For tuna:

- 6 tbsp/90 mL extra-virgin olive oil
- ¼ medium Vidalia onion, thinly sliced
- 2 cloves garlic, peeled and lightly crushed
- 1 bay leaf
- 2 tbsp/30 mL sherry vinegar
- 2 tbsp/30 mL dry white wine
- ¼ tsp/1 mL dried basil
- ¼ tsp/1 mL dried thyme
- 2 sprigs parsley
- 4 peppercorns
- 2 cloves
-   Kosher or sea salt
- 8 oz/225 g boneless, skinless tuna steak

For vegetables:

- 1 small eggplant
- 1 red bell pepper (capsicum)
- 1 green bell pepper (capsicum)
- 1 medium Vidalia onion, peeled
- 1 tbsp/15 mL extra-virgin olive oil
-   Freshly squeezed lemon juice to taste
- 1 tbsp/15 mL minced parsley
- 1 tsp/5 mL minced fresh thyme leaves
-   Kosher or sea salt
-   Freshly ground pepper

To prepare the tuna, heat the oil in a small skillet over medium heat and sauté the onion, garlic, and bay leaf until the onion is softened, pressing on the garlic cloves with a wooden spoon to release their flavor. Add the vinegar, wine, basil, thyme, parsley, peppercorns, cloves, and salt to taste. Bring to a boil over high heat. Reduce the heat to medium-low, then cover and simmer for 30 minutes for flavors to blend.

Add the tuna, spooning some of the sauce over it. Cover and simmer for about 10 minutes, turning once, until tuna is firm. Remove from the heat and let cool. Transfer the tuna, cooking liquid, and flavorings to a shallow dish. Cover and refrigerate for 24 hours.

To prepare the vegetables, preheat the oven to 500°F/260°C. Put the eggplant, red and green peppers, and onion in a roasting pan and roast for 30–40 minutes, turning once, until skins are charred and vegetables are tender. Remove from the oven and put in a deep dish. Cover with foil and let stand for 15 minutes.

Peel the skin from the eggplant. Cut the eggplant in half and scrape out most of the seeds. Peel the skin from the peppers, discarding stems and seeds. Cut the eggplant, peppers, and onion into 1-inch/2.5 cm strips and toss together on a serving platter. Drizzle with the olive oil and lemon juice, and sprinkle with the parsley, thyme, and salt and pepper to taste. Toss well. Cut the tuna into bite-size pieces and arrange on top of the vegetables. ◎

Pescado A La Sal

Whole Fish Baked in Salt

Baking whole fish under a dome of coarse salt, which acts as an insulator, results in incredibly succulent fish that's not at all salty. It is important to leave the scales intact as these keep the fish moist but block the salt from penetrating the flesh. Sea salt with grains the size of pebbles is best, but somewhat finer kosher salt may also be used. Salpicón sauce is a popular Spanish dipping sauce for fish or shellfish.

Makes 4 servings

For salpicón sauce:

¾ cup/175 mL extra-virgin olive oil

6 tbsp/90 mL red wine vinegar

5 drained cornichon pickles, chopped

2 tbsp/30 mL minced Vidalia onion

2 tbsp/30 mL drained capers

2 tbsp/30 mL chopped pimiento

1 tbsp/15 mL minced parsley

Kosher or sea salt

Freshly ground pepper

For fish:

½ tsp/2 mL each dried marjoram, oregano, rosemary, and thyme

2 1¾-lb/875 g whole fish, such as red snapper, cleaned but heads and scales left on

4 sprigs parsley

2 bay leaves

4 cups/1 L very coarse sea salt or kosher salt

Extra-virgin olive oil for brushing

Homemade or good-quality prepared mayonnaise to serve

To prepare the salpicón sauce, stir together the oil, vinegar, pickles, onion, capers, pimiento, parsley, and salt and pepper to taste in a small serving bowl. Set aside.

To prepare the fish, preheat the oven to 400°F/200°C. Stir together the marjoram, oregano, rosemary, and thyme in a small bowl. Sprinkle the herb mixture into the cavities of the fish, and add the parsley and bay leaves.

In a large bowl, stir together the salt and 2 tbsp/30 mL water. Sprinkle a thin layer of salt over the bottom of a shallow baking dish just large enough to hold both fish side by side. Arrange the fish on the salt and brush with olive oil. Spoon the remaining salt over the fish to cover them completely, patting it so that it adheres to the fish (you may not need all of the salt).

Bake, uncovered, for about 20 minutes or until a meat thermometer inserted into the thickest part of the fish registers 145°F/63°C. Tap the salt crust lightly with a meat mallet to crack it. Lift off and discard the crust. Transfer the fish to a cutting board. Brush off any remaining salt and peel off the skin from the upper side of each fish. Fillet the fish, removing the heads and back bones, and transfer the fillets to a warm platter. Serve with the salpicón sauce and mayonnaise. ◎

Pudin De Merluza

Chilled Fish Terrine with Capers and Mayonnaise

This light fish terrine, typically prepared with hake or cod, makes a refreshing summer meal. It was first introduced to me by my Spanish mother-in-law many years ago, and has been a warm-weather staple in my household ever since.

Makes 6 servings

1 tbsp/15 mL extra-virgin olive oil	2 tbsp/30 mL tomato sauce
1 medium Vidalia onion, finely chopped	1 drained piquillo pepper, finely chopped
1 carrot, finely chopped	5 eggs
1 cup/250 mL dry white wine	3 tbsp/45 mL heavy (whipping) cream
2 cups/500 mL clam juice	Freshly ground pepper
2 sprigs parsley	Freshly grated nutmeg to taste
1 bay leaf	1 tbsp/15 mL drained small capers
Pinch of crumbled saffron threads	Homemade or good-quality prepared mayonnaise to serve
Kosher or sea salt	
1 lb/500 g cod steaks	
2 ½-inch/1 cm slices firm-textured French-style bread, crusts removed	

Heat the oil in a large skillet over medium heat and sauté the onion and carrot until the onion is softened. Add the wine and bring to a boil over high heat. Boil until the liquid has reduced by half. Add the clam juice, parsley, bay leaf, saffron, and salt to taste, and bring to a boil. Add the cod steaks then reduce the heat to medium-low. Cover and simmer for 20 minutes or until the fish flakes easily with a fork.

With a slotted spoon, remove cod to a shallow dish. Strain the cooking liquid through a fine sieve, discarding solids and reserving ¾ cup/175 mL liquid. When the cod is cool enough to handle, remove any skin and bones then shred the fish finely with your fingers.

In a medium bowl, soak the bread in the reserved cooking liquid until it disintegrates. Add the shredded cod, tomato sauce, and piquillo pepper. In a separate medium bowl, beat the eggs lightly with the cream, then add to the fish mixture, along with salt, pepper, and nutmeg to taste, being generous with the nutmeg.

Pour the fish mixture into a well-greased 9 x 5-inch/2 L loaf pan. Cover the pan tightly with foil and set in a shallow flameproof roasting pan. Pour the boiling water into the roasting pan to come halfway up sides of the loaf pan. Cook over medium heat for about 1½ hours or until fish loaf is set. Remove the loaf pan from the water and loosen the foil but leave it in place. Let the terrine cool slightly at room temperature, then refrigerate until cold. To serve, unmold the terrine onto a cutting board and cut crosswise into slices. Arrange the slices on a serving platter and garnish with capers. Serve with mayonnaise. ◎

Poultry and Game

Pollo Del Día Anterior

Yesterday's Chicken

In this recipe the chicken cooks then marinates in oil, onion, garlic, bay leaf, and vinegar (known as an *escabeche* sauce). It can be reheated before serving, although I prefer it at room temperature, along with a salad and little new potatoes that have been peeled, boiled, and cooled.

Makes 4 servings

1	3–3½-lb/1.5–1.7 kg chicken	¼	cup/50 mL dry white wine
	Kosher or sea salt	3	tbsp/45 mL red wine vinegar
	Freshly ground pepper	2	tbsp/30 mL minced parsley
6	tbsp/90 mL extra-virgin olive oil	2	tsp/10 mL minced fresh thyme leaves or ¼ tsp/1 mL dried thyme
2	medium Vidalia onions, halved crosswise		
5	cloves garlic, peeled and lightly crushed	10	peppercorns
2	tbsp/30 mL minced shallots		Pinch of crumbled saffron threads
3	bay leaves	3	eggs
¾	cup/175 mL chicken broth		All-purpose flour for dusting

Cut the wings and legs off the chicken. Cut off and discard the wing tips and the bony ends of the legs. Cut each breast and thigh in half crosswise with sturdy kitchen shears. Sprinkle the chicken pieces with salt and pepper, and set aside at room temperature for 10 minutes.

Heat ¼ cup/50 mL oil in a large skillet over medium heat and sauté the chicken pieces until browned on all sides. Add the onions, garlic, shallots, bay leaves, and salt to taste. Stir in the broth, wine, vinegar, parsley, thyme, peppercorns, and saffron (the liquid should barely cover the chicken). Bring to a boil over high heat. Simmer, covered, for 45 minutes. Remove the chicken to a platter, cover and refrigerate. Pour the contents of the skillet into a medium bowl, cover and refrigerate until chilled. Remove the fat from the surface.

Beat the eggs in a shallow bowl. Heat the remaining oil in a large shallow flameproof casserole over medium-high heat. Dust the chicken pieces with flour, then coat with the beaten egg. Cook the chicken pieces, turning often, until browned on all sides.

Meanwhile, reheat the reserved cooking liquid in a medium saucepan over medium heat. Strain the hot cooking liquid over the chicken. Bring to a boil over high heat. Simmer for 2 minutes, then remove from the heat and let cool. Cover and refrigerate for at least several hours or up to 3 days. Serve at room temperature or reheated. ⊕

Pavo Guisado Al Estilo De Faín

Turkey Fricassee Faín

This turkey fricassee, or stew, is among my very favorite dishes when made with the free-range turkeys that are raised in western Andalucía at the tranquil Faín estate, splendidly set amidst olive groves.

Because turkey bones are almost impossible to cut, I advise having a butcher hack or saw the turkey parts into a manageable size (a medium-sized chicken will also work well). The sauce is exceptionally delicious, and once more it is dried sweet red pepper (*ñora*) that makes all the difference. Serve with a green salad.

Makes 4 servings

3–3½ lb/1.5–1.7 kg turkey (or chicken) pieces, such as wings, drumsticks and/or thighs, sawed into 2-inch/5 cm pieces, discarding the wing tips and bony ends of the drumsticks

   Kosher or sea salt

2 tbsp/30 mL extra-virgin olive oil

1 medium Vidalia onion, thinly sliced

2 cloves garlic, minced

1 small dried sweet red pepper (*ñora*), or ½ dried New Mexico chile, stems and seeds removed, and pepper crumbled

1 medium tomato, chopped

1 tbsp/15 mL minced parsley

¾ cup/175 mL chicken broth

½ cup/125 mL dry white wine

¼ tsp/1 mL ground cumin

3 peppercorns

   Pinch of crumbled saffron threads

Sprinkle the turkey pieces with salt. Heat the oil in a large shallow flameproof casserole over medium-high heat, and sauté the turkey pieces until brown on all sides. Add the onion, garlic, and dried pepper, and sauté until the onion is softened. Stir in the tomato and parsley, and sauté for about 2 minutes. Add the broth, wine, cumin, peppercorns, and saffron. Bring to a boil over high heat. Cover and simmer for 1¼ hours until turkey is tender and is no longer pink inside. Serve straight from the casserole. ✢

Pollo Al Ajillo

Chicken in Garlic Sauce

The variations on this Spanish favorite are endless, but no matter which recipe is used—simply fried in olive oil with plenty of garlic, or with a touch of wine, vinegar or saffron—it is a dish that never fails to please.

Makes 4 servings

1	3–3½-lb/1.5–1.7 kg chicken	2	cloves garlic, minced
	Kosher or sea salt	1	tbsp/15 mL dry white wine
	Freshly ground pepper	1	tbsp/15 mL chicken broth
	Olive oil for frying	1	tsp/5 mL red wine vinegar
1	small whole head garlic, divided into cloves, and lightly crushed		Pinch of crumbled saffron threads

Cut the wings and legs off the chicken. Cut off and discard the wing tips and the bony ends of the legs. Cut each breast and thigh in half crosswise with sturdy kitchen shears. Sprinkle the chicken pieces with salt and pepper, and set aside at room temperature for 10 minutes.

Pour the oil into a large skillet to a depth of ¼–½ inch/5 mm–1 cm, and heat over high heat. Add the chicken and whole garlic cloves and cook for about 12 minutes, shaking the skillet and turning the chicken pieces often, until they are golden brown and no longer pink inside. Drain the chicken through a metal strainer, discarding the oil and the garlic cloves.

In the same skillet, combine the minced garlic, wine, broth, vinegar, saffron, and a pinch of salt. Bring to a boil over medium-high heat. Add the chicken pieces to the skillet and toss until the liquid has been absorbed. Transfer to a serving platter. ⊕

Pollo Chilindrón

Chicken with Tomatoes and Piquillo Peppers

Chicken braised with tomatoes, peppers, and onions is an incredibly delicious blend of flavors from the region of Aragón. Here the dish is highlighted by a touch of Serrano ham, Spanish smoked paprika, and dried red chile pepper.

Makes 4 servings

1	3–3½-lb/1.5–1.7 kg chicken
	Kosher or sea salt
2	tbsp/30 mL extra-virgin olive oil
1	small Vidalia onion, chopped
2	cloves garlic, minced
2	tbsp/30 mL chopped Serrano ham or prosciutto
½	tsp/2 mL sweet paprika, preferably Spanish smoked

2	small plum (Roma) tomatoes, chopped
4	drained piquillo peppers, cut into ½-inch/1 cm strips
1	1-inch/2.5 cm piece dried red chile pepper (such as Spanish *guindilla* or *guajillo*), seeds removed
	Freshly ground pepper
	Chicken broth or water as required

Cut the wings and legs off the chicken. Cut off and discard the wing tips and the bony ends of the legs. Cut each breast and thigh in half crosswise with sturdy kitchen shears. Sprinkle the chicken pieces with salt, and set aside at room temperature for 10 minutes.

Heat the oil in a large shallow flameproof casserole over medium-high heat and sauté the chicken pieces until golden on all sides. Add the onion and garlic, and sauté until the onion is softened. Add the ham and cook for 1 minute, then stir in the paprika. Add the tomatoes, and cook for 1 minute. Stir in the piquillo peppers, chile pepper, and salt and pepper to taste. Cover and simmer for 45 minutes or until the juices run clear when chicken is pierced, adding a little broth or water if stew seems too dry. Serve straight from the casserole. ✤

Pollo De Corral Con Patatas

Stewed Chicken with Potatoes

In the mountain-ringed town of Compludo in the province of León, chickens wander the streets at will—free-range in its truest sense—and villagers naturally cook with local ingredients readily at hand. Compludo is in the fertile region of El Bierzo, famed for its fruits and vegetables, and its superior wines. This recipe makes use of the village chickens and locally grown onions, carrots, peppers, and potatoes, as well as the native red wine, which is becoming increasingly well known. The sauce is exceptional, and the potatoes the best I have ever eaten. All that is needed to complete this meal is a green salad.

Makes 4 servings

1	3–3½-lb/1.5–1.7 kg chicken	6	tbsp/90 mL extra-virgin olive oil
	Kosher or sea salt	1	medium Vidalia onion, finely chopped
	Freshly ground pepper	1	medium red bell pepper (capsicum), seeded and finely chopped
2	tbsp/30 mL minced parsley	½	cup/125 mL finely chopped carrots
1	tbsp/15 mL minced fresh thyme leaves or ½ tsp/2 mL dried thyme	1	small tomato, finely chopped
2	cloves garlic, minced	2	tbsp/30 mL chopped Serrano ham or prosciutto
½	tsp/2 mL sweet paprika, preferably Spanish smoked	1	large baking potato, peeled and cut into ½-inch/1 cm cubes
1¼	cups/300 mL dry red wine		
1	bay leaf		

Cut the wings and legs off the chicken. Cut off and discard the wing tips and the bony ends of the legs. Cut each breast and thigh in half crosswise with sturdy kitchen shears. Sprinkle the chicken pieces with salt and pepper, and set aside at room temperature for 10 minutes.

Mash the parsley, thyme, garlic, and a pinch of salt to a paste in a large mortar. Mash in the paprika, then stir in the wine and bay leaf, and set aside.

Heat 3 tbsp/45 mL oil in a shallow flameproof casserole over medium-high heat, and sauté the chicken pieces until golden on all sides. Add the onion, red pepper, carrots, tomato, and ham, and sauté until the vegetables are softened. Stir in the mortar mixture and bring to a boil over high heat. Simmer, covered, for 30 minutes.

Meanwhile, heat the remaining oil in a large skillet over medium heat. Add the potato in a single layer, sprinkle with salt, and sauté for 2 minutes, turning with a metal spatula to prevent sticking. Reduce heat to medium-low and cook, covered, for about 10 minutes until potato is tender, turning occasionally with the spatula. Drain off the oil, add the potatoes to the chicken and cook for 5 minutes until chicken is no longer pink inside. ✣

Guiso Caldoso De Aldea Antigua

Chicken and Sparerib Stew

This exceptional village recipe from northwestern Spain filled my kitchen with the same enticing aromas that greet you at midday in little Spanish towns. The additions of saffron and cumin, and the mixture of pork ribs, pancetta, and chicken, give the stew a distinctive flavor. Have your butcher saw the ribs into pieces.

Makes 6–8 servings

2 tbsp/30 mL extra-virgin olive oil	1 medium carrot, finely chopped
1 lb/500 g pork spareribs or baby back ribs, sawed lengthwise into 2-inch/5 cm strips, then each strip cut into 2-rib pieces	4 garlic cloves, minced
	¼ cup/50 mL minced parsley
Kosher or sea salt	4 small (2-inch/5 cm diameter) new potatoes, scrubbed and halved
Freshly ground pepper	¼ cup/50 mL dry white wine
½ cup/125 mL chicken broth	1 bay leaf
1 3–3½-lb/1.5–1.7 kg chicken	½ cup/125 mL fresh or frozen peas
1 4-oz/120 g piece pancettta, cut into ¾-inch/1.5 cm cubes	¼ tsp/1 mL ground cumin
1 medium Vidalia onion, finely chopped	Pinch of crumbled saffron threads

Heat 1 tbsp/15 mL oil in a large shallow flameproof casserole and sauté the pork ribs until brown, sprinkling them with salt and pepper as they cook. Stir in the broth and ⅓ cup/75 mL water. Bring to a boil over high heat. Cover and simmer for 1 hour. (The ribs can be prepared in advance.)

Cut the wings and legs off the chicken. Cut off and discard the wing tips and the bony ends of the legs. Cut each breast and thigh in half crosswise with sturdy kitchen shears. Sprinkle the chicken pieces with salt and pepper, and set aside at room temperature for 10 minutes.

Remove the ribs from the casserole. Measure 1½ cups/375 mL cooking liquid, adding water if necessary. Skim off and discard any fat from the cooking liquid. Wipe out the casserole.

Heat the remaining oil in the casserole over medium-high heat, and sauté the chicken pieces and pancetta until browned on all sides. Add the onion, carrot, garlic, and parsley and sauté until the vegetables are starting to soften.

Return the ribs and broth to the casserole, along with the potatoes, wine, and bay leaf. Bring to a boil over high heat. Cover and simmer for 25 minutes. Stir in the peas, cumin, saffron, and salt and pepper to taste. Cover and simmer for 15 minutes until the potatoes are tender and the chicken is no longer pink inside. Serve in shallow bowls. ⊕

Pato A La Sevillana

Duck with Olives in Sherry Sauce

The tantalizing earthy flavor of this duck is a result of the Andalusian blend of olives and sherry. In southern Spain, dry *fino* sherry is naturally poured to accompany such tapas as olives and Spanish ham. It also contributes to a wonderful sauce for duck that brings to life the flavors of Andalucía and is commonly referred to as "Sevilla style."

Makes 4 servings

4	cloves garlic	½	cup/125 mL chicken broth
1	4½-lb/2.2 kg duck or 3–3½-lb/ 1.5–1.7 kg chicken	½	cup/125 mL dry (*fino*) sherry
2	slices Vidalia onion	2	carrots, thinly sliced
½	cup/125 mL dry white wine	1½	tsp/7 mL minced fresh thyme leaves or ¼ tsp/1 mL dried thyme
½	cup/125 mL pitted and coarsely chopped green Spanish olives	1	bay leaf
2	tbsp/30 mL extra-virgin olive oil	1	sprig parsley
1	medium Vidalia onion, chopped	4	peppercorns
			Kosher or sea salt

Preheat the oven to 350°F/180°C. Peel the cloves of garlic, mince 2 of them and set aside. Put the 2 whole garlic cloves in the duck's cavity, along with the onion slices. Truss the duck and prick it deeply all over with a fork. Put the duck in a roasting pan, along with the neck, if available, and roast, uncovered, for about 1 hour, until juices run clear when leg is pierced. Leave the oven on.

Remove the duck to a board and cut it into quarters. Pour off all the fat from the roasting pan. Add ¼ cup/50 mL wine to the pan and bring to a boil over medium heat, stirring to scrape up any browned bits from the bottom of the pan. Reserve these pan juices and discard the neck.

Put the olives in a small saucepan with the remaining wine. Bring to a boil over high heat and boil for 5 minutes. Drain, discarding the wine, and set the olives aside.

Heat the oil in a large shallow flameproof casserole over medium heat. Add the chopped onion and the remaining garlic, and sauté until the onion is softened. Add the broth, sherry, carrots, thyme, bay leaf, parsley, peppercorns, the reserved pan juices, and salt to taste. Bring to a boil over high heat. Simmer for 5 minutes. Add the duck pieces, spooning some of the sauce over them. Cover the casserole, transfer it to the oven, and cook for 45 minutes.

Remove the duck to a serving platter. Strain the sauce into a medium saucepan, pressing on the solids with the back of a metal soup ladle to extract as much liquid as possible. Add a few tablespoons of water to the casserole and bring to a boil over medium heat, stirring to scrape up any browned bits from the bottom of the casserole. Add these juices to the sauce. Stir in the olives, reheat the sauce, and pour over the duck before serving. ⊕

Higadillos De Pollo Al Jerez

Chicken Livers in Sherry Sauce

A dish from western Andalucía—Spain's Sherry Triangle—that incorporates truffles, mushrooms, green olives, and a hint of local sherry, all of which give a special flavor and a touch of elegance to these chicken livers.

Makes 4 servings

- 1 lb/500 g chicken livers
- 3 tbsp/45 mL (approx.) unsalted butter
- Kosher or sea salt
- 3 large scallions, chopped
- 4½ tsp/22 mL all-purpose flour
- ¾ cup/175 mL plus 3 tbsp/45 mL chicken broth
- 3 tbsp/45 mL dry (*fino*) sherry
- 6 medium cremini mushrooms, brushed clean, and halved or quartered

- 1 tbsp/15 mL chopped truffle (optional)
- Freshly ground pepper
- 1 tbsp/15 mL pitted and minced green Spanish olives
- 1 tbsp/15 mL minced hard-cooked egg yolk
- 1 tbsp/15 mL minced parsley

Pick over the livers and cut each in half. Heat 3 tbsp/45 mL butter in a shallow flameproof casserole over medium heat, and brown the livers quickly (they will cook a little more later). Remove to a large plate and sprinkle with salt.

Add the scallions to the butter remaining in the casserole, adding a little more butter if necessary, and sauté until softened. Stir in the flour, then gradually whisk in the broth and sherry, and cook, stirring constantly, until the sauce is smooth and has thickened. Add the mushrooms, truffle, and salt and pepper to taste. Cover and simmer for 5 minutes.

Return the livers to the casserole and cook for 2–3 minutes (they should still be slightly pink inside). Spoon the livers and their sauce onto a serving platter. Serve garnished with the olives, egg yolk, and parsley. ⊕

Pularda A La Suprema De Trufas

Stewing Chicken with Cream and Truffles

Plebeian boiled chicken becomes a sophisticated dish with a haunting flavor when cream and truffles are added. The recipe may not seem like typical Spanish country fare, but in bucolic Artiés in northern Catalunya, where cows graze and truffles grow, local cooking can sometimes be most refined.

Makes 5–6 servings

1	4½–5-lb/2.2–2.5 kg chicken, with neck if possible	10	peppercorns
5½	cups/1.3 L chicken broth	2	bay leaves
⅔	cup/150 mL dry white wine		Kosher or sea salt
2	medium carrots, finely chopped	2	tbsp/30 mL unsalted butter
1	medium leek, (white part only), finely chopped	2	tbsp/30 mL all-purpose flour
1	medium Vidalia onion, finely chopped	2	tbsp/30 mL heavy (whipping) cream
4	sprigs parsley	4	jarred truffles, drained and finely chopped
4	sprigs fresh thyme or ½ tsp/2 mL dried thyme	2	tsp/10 mL truffle juice (from jar)

Put the chicken and its neck in a large deep pot and add the broth, wine, carrots, leek, onion, parsley, thyme, peppercorns, bay leaves, and salt to taste. Bring to a boil over high heat, skimming off any foam. Cover and simmer for 1½ hours until juices run clear when leg is pierced.

Transfer the chicken to a warm platter and cut it into quarters, discarding the neck, wing bones, wing tips, and the skin. Remove the breasts from the ribs, discarding the ribs.

Strain the broth into a measuring cup; you should have 2¼ cups/550 mL. (If there's more, return the broth to the pot and boil until it is reduced.) Return the chicken to the empty pot, and pour in ¼ cup/50 mL reserved broth. Keep warm over low heat.

Melt the butter in a medium saucepan over medium heat. Add the flour and cook for 1 minute, stirring constantly. Stir in the cream, then gradually whisk in the remaining broth, the truffles, and the truffle juice. Cook, stirring constantly, until the sauce is smooth and has thickened. Transfer the chicken to a serving platter and pour the sauce over it. ⊕

Pollo Al Vino Blanco Con Cilantro

Chicken with White Wine, Grape Juice, and Cilantro

It's not surprising that this great chicken preparation from Andalucía has a hint of sweetness and a punch of cilantro—that's the Moorish influence, which is still palpable in southern Spain. Contrary to popular thinking, cilantro is not Mexican but originated in Egypt; it traveled to Spain by way of the Moors, then the Spanish took it to the New World.

Makes 4 servings

1 3–3½-lb/1.5–1.7 kg chicken	¾ cup/175 mL dry white wine
Kosher or sea salt	⅓ cup/75 mL white grape juice
Freshly ground pepper	¼ cup/50 mL chopped Serrano ham or prosciutto
3 tbsp/45 mL extra-virgin olive oil	
1 small Vidalia onion, thinly sliced	6 tbsp/90 mL minced cilantro

Cut the wings and legs off the chicken. Cut off and discard the wing tips and the bony ends of the legs. Cut each breast and thigh in half crosswise with sturdy kitchen shears. Sprinkle the chicken pieces with salt and pepper, and set aside at room temperature for 10 minutes.

Heat the oil in a large shallow flameproof casserole over medium-high heat, and sauté the chicken until golden on all sides. Add the onion and sauté until softened. Stir in the wine, grape juice, ham, and 3 tbsp/45 mL cilantro. Bring to a boil over high heat. Cover and simmer for 45 minutes until juices run clear when chicken is pierced.

Remove the chicken to a warm platter. Boil the contents of the casserole until the sauce is reduced and slightly thickened. Drizzle the sauce over the chicken and garnish with the remaining cilantro. ⊕

Pollo Al Coñac

Braised Chicken in Brandy Sauce

A good amount of garlic mellowed by long cooking helps to produce a moist, tender, and unusually tasty chicken.

Makes 4 servings

1 3–3½-lb/1.5–1.7 kg chicken	⅔ cup/150 mL dry white wine
Kosher or sea salt	¼ cup/50 mL chicken broth
All-purpose flour for dusting	1 bay leaf
2 tbsp/30 mL extra-virgin olive oil	Pinch of crumbled saffron threads
2 medium Vidalia onions, finely chopped	1 whole head garlic, loose skin removed
3 tbsp/45 mL brandy	

Cut the wings and legs off the chicken. Cut off and discard the wing tips and the bony ends of the legs. Cut each breast and thigh in half crosswise with sturdy kitchen shears. Sprinkle the chicken pieces with salt, then dust with flour.

Heat the oil in a large shallow flameproof casserole over medium-high heat, and sauté the chicken until golden on all sides. Add the onions and sauté until softened.

Standing back, add the brandy and ignite it. When the flames die down, stir in the wine, broth, bay leaf, saffron, and salt to taste. Slash the head of garlic almost but not quite through vertically and add to the casserole. Bring to a boil over high heat. Cover and simmer for about 40 minutes until juices run clear when chicken is pierced. Remove the head of garlic and squeeze the garlic cloves into the sauce, discarding the skin. Serve straight from the casserole. ⊕

Pollo Al Romero Con Limón Y Piñones

Lemon Chicken with Rosemary and Pine Nuts

This excellent recipe for sautéed chicken in a lemon, rosemary, and pine nut sauce has its origins in past centuries. In fact, I've found several recipes that are practically identical to this one, except the older recipes add ginger, a medieval touch that highlights the lemon tang of the sauce.

Makes 4 servings

1	3–3½- lb/1.5–1.7 kg chicken	¼	cup/50 mL dry white wine
	Kosher or sea salt	½	lemon, cut into thin wedges
2	tbsp/30 mL extra-virgin olive oil	2	tbsp/30 mL minced parsley
1	medium Vidalia onion, finely chopped	3	sprigs rosemary
2	tbsp/30 mL chopped Serrano ham or prosciutto	½	tsp/2 mL peeled and grated fresh ginger
2	tbsp/30 mL pine nuts	1	bay leaf, crumbled
1	clove garlic, minced		Pinch of crumbled saffron threads
½	cup/125 mL chicken broth		Freshly ground pepper

Cut the wings and legs off the chicken. Cut off and discard the wing tips and the bony ends of the legs. Cut each breast and thigh in half crosswise with sturdy kitchen shears. Sprinkle the chicken pieces with salt, and set aside at room temperature for 10 minutes.

Heat the oil in a large shallow flameproof casserole over medium-high heat, and sauté the chicken until golden on all sides. Add the onion, ham, pine nuts, and garlic, and sauté until the onion is softened. Add the broth and wine. Squeeze the lemon wedges over the chicken, then scatter the wedges over the top. Add the parsley, rosemary, ginger, bay leaf, saffron, and pepper to taste. Bring to a boil over high heat. Cover and simmer for 45 minutes until juices run clear when chicken is pierced. Serve straight from the casserole. ⊕

Conejo En Salmorejo
Rabbit in Spicy Wine and Vinegar Sauce

Mesón El Drago, a restaurant set in a charmingly old country house with terracotta floors and wood-beamed ceilings on the island of Tenerife, takes its name from the impressive dragon tree—a phantasmagorical tree indigenous to Spain's Canary Islands—that grows on its patio. Here you will find wonderful renditions of traditional island dishes, including this rabbit, piquant with vinegar. You may substitute chicken but the results are far better with rabbit.

Makes 4 servings

½ dried sweet red pepper (ñora), or ¼ dried New Mexico chile, stem and seeds removed

8 cloves garlic, minced

1 tsp/5 mL kosher or sea salt

½ cup/125 mL red wine vinegar

2 tbsp/30 mL sweet paprika, preferably Spanish smoked

1½ cups/375 mL dry white wine

⅔ cup/150 mL extra-virgin olive oil

2 tsp/10 mL minced fresh oregano leaves or ¼ tsp/1 mL dried oregano

2 tsp/10 mL minced fresh thyme leaves or ¼ tsp/1 mL dried thyme

1 2½–3-lb/1.2–1.5 kg rabbit, cut in small serving pieces

Crumble the dried pepper into a mortar and mash to a paste with the garlic and salt. Stir in the vinegar and paprika, and transfer to a bowl large enough to hold the rabbit. Stir in the wine, ½ cup/125 mL oil, the oregano, and thyme. Add the rabbit pieces, turning to coat well. Cover and refrigerate for 2 hours.

Drain the rabbit pieces, reserving the marinade, and pat the rabbit pieces dry on paper towels. Heat the remaining oil in a large shallow flameproof casserole over medium-high heat, and sauté the rabbit pieces until golden on all sides. Remove the rabbit pieces to a large plate and pour off the oil from the casserole. Pour the marinade into the casserole and bring to a boil over high heat. Boil until the liquid has reduced by half. Season with salt to taste. Return the rabbit pieces to the casserole. Cover and simmer 1 hour until rabbit is tender. Serve straight from the casserole. ⊕

Caldereta De Codornices
Potted Quail

Quite by chance we stopped for lunch at an unprepossessing restaurant in the town of Santa María in northern Spain. The dining room was filled with locals, all eating this potted quail, a simple but quite delicious dish of the day. The slight sweetness of the incredibly good sauce is a result of the large amount of onion—the sauce has little else and there is minimal liquid except for what the onion produces in the tightly covered stew pot.

Makes 4 servings

8	quail, trussed	2	tbsp/30 mL brandy
	Kosher or sea salt	2	tbsp/30 mL red wine vinegar
2	tbsp/30 mL extra-virgin olive oil	3	sprigs parsley
2	medium Vidalia onions, coarsely chopped	1	bay leaf
3	cloves garlic, minced	6	peppercorns

Sprinkle the quail with salt. Heat 1 tbsp/15 mL oil in a large deep pot and brown the quail on all sides. Add the onions and garlic, drizzle in the remaining oil and sauté until the onions are softened.

Standing back, add the brandy and ignite it. When the flames die down, stir in the vinegar, parsley, bay leaf, peppercorns, and salt to taste. Cover tightly and simmer for 1 hour until the quail are very tender. Transfer quail and their sauce to a serving platter. ⊕

Meat

Entrecot Al Queso Cabrales

Steak with Spanish Blue Cheese Sauce

This dish comes from the northern region of Asturias, where local blue cheese called *Cabrales* is aged in mountain caves, then wrapped in tree leaves. When the cheese is transformed into a sauce to pour over steak, the match is ideal.

Makes 4 servings

4 oz/120 g *Cabrales* or Gorgonzola cheese, crumbled	Freshly ground pepper
1 tbsp/15 mL minced parsley	1 tbsp/15 mL unsalted butter
1 clove garlic, minced	1 tsp/5 mL extra-virgin olive oil
4 tsp/20 mL dry white wine	4 rib steaks, about 1 inch/2.5 cm thick
1 tsp/5 mL freshly squeezed lemon juice	¼ cup/50 mL chicken broth or water
Pinch of sweet paprika, preferably Spanish smoked	Kosher or sea salt

In the top of a double boiler or in a heatproof bowl set over a saucepan of simmering water, combine the cheese, parsley, garlic, wine, lemon juice, paprika, and pepper to taste. Cook, stirring occasionally, until the sauce is smooth and heated through. Set aside and keep warm.

Melt the butter with the oil in a large heavy skillet over medium-high heat just until the butter starts to brown. Add the steaks and cook for 6–8 minutes, turning once, or until done to taste. Remove the steaks to a warm platter and keep warm.

Add the broth to the skillet and bring to a boil over high heat, stirring to scrape up any browned bits from the bottom of the skillet. Stir 2 tbsp/30 mL of these pan juices into the cheese sauce, then season the sauce with salt to taste. Pour the sauce over the steaks and serve at once. ▣

Cocido Madrileño

Boiled Beef and Chickpea Dinner

The ultimate one-pot meal in Spain. Over the centuries cocido became a staple of the Spanish, and each region today has its own version, none more famous and beloved than cocido *Madrileño*. The flavorful broth is served first—usually with fine noodles—then is followed by platters of vegetables and meats, accompanied by sautéed cabbage (p. 151). Start preparing the dish a day ahead.

Makes 8 servings

2 cups/500 mL dried chickpeas	Kosher or sea salt
1 2½-lb/1.2 kg beef chuck or blade roast	Freshly ground pepper
2 ham or beef bones	4 medium new potatoes, scrubbed
2 bone-in, skin-on chicken thighs	2 large carrots
8 oz/225 g sweet chorizo	1 Vidalia onion, halved
1 4-oz/120 g piece slab bacon	1 leek (white part only)
1 4-oz/120 g piece Serrano ham	2 cloves garlic, peeled
4 oz/120 g *morcilla* (Spanish blood sausage)	4 oz/120 g very fine noodles

The day before serving, put the chickpeas in a large bowl and add enough cold water to cover them. Let stand overnight. Put the beef, ham bones, chicken, chorizo, bacon, ham, *morcilla*, and salt and pepper to taste in a large pot. Pour in 18 cups/4.5 L water. Bring to a boil over high heat, skimming off any foam. Cover and simmer for 1½ hours. Let cool, then refrigerate.

The following day, remove the fat that has solidified on the top of the cooked meats. Drain the chickpeas, tie them in a net bag or a double layer of cheesecloth, and add them to the pot. Add the potatoes, carrots, onion, leek, and garlic to the pot. Bring to a boil over high heat. Season with salt and pepper to taste. Cover and simmer for 3½ hours until the chickpeas are tender.

Remove the bag of chickpeas. Strain the broth, reserving the meats and vegetables, and discarding the ham bones. Cut the meats, potatoes, carrots, onion, and leek into serving portions and arrange, with the chickpeas, on a warm platter. Keep warm.

Return the broth to the pot and bring to a boil over high heat. Add the noodles and cook for 6–8 minutes until al dente. Ladle the broth into soup bowls and serve as a first course, followed by meats, vegetables, and chickpeas. 🔲

Guisado Al Estilo De Coto Doñana

Beef Stew with Cumin and Coriander

Coto Doñana is a unique and immense area of virgin sands, dunes, marshland, and pines in south-western Spain that teems with wildlife and migratory birds. Coriander is a spice (its leaf is cilantro) that thrives in Doñana, and the cumin and coriander that season this fragrant stew are a heritage of the Moors, and frequently appear in Andalusian cooking. Very small boiled white potatoes are a nice accompaniment.

Makes 4 servings

2 tbsp/30 mL extra-virgin olive oil	1½ tsp/7 mL ground cumin
1½–2 lb/750 g–1 kg boneless stew beef, cut into 1-inch/2.5 cm cubes	1½ tsp/7 mL ground coriander
Kosher or sea salt	½ tsp/2 mL crushed hot red chile flakes, or to taste
2 medium Vidalia onions, thinly sliced	4 sprigs fresh thyme or ½ tsp/2 mL dried thyme
4 cloves garlic, minced	2 sprigs parsley
3 medium tomatoes, finely chopped	¼ cup/50 mL low-sodium beef broth
3 tbsp/45 mL minced cilantro	¼ cup/50 mL dry (*fino*) sherry

Heat the oil in a large shallow flameproof casserole over medium-high heat, and brown the beef, sprinkling it with salt as it cooks. Add the onions and garlic to the casserole, and sauté until the onion has softened. Stir in the tomatoes, 2 tbsp/30 mL cilantro, 1 tsp/5 mL cumin, the coriander, chile flakes, thyme, and parsley, and sauté for 2 minutes. Add the broth, sherry, and ¼ cup/50 mL water. Bring to a boil over high heat. Cover and simmer for 1½ hours.

Stir in the remaining cumin and simmer for 30 minutes until the beef is tender. Serve straight from the casserole, sprinkled with the remaining cilantro. ▣

Estofado De Vaca Con Setas Y Piquillos

Beef Stew with Mushrooms and Piquillo Peppers

This exceptional stew contains simple ingredients, but Spain's piquillo peppers lend their unique flavor and a most appealing splash of color.

Makes 4–6 servings

2   tbsp/30 mL extra-virgin olive oil

2   lb/1 kg boneless stew beef, cut into 1-inch/2.5 cm cubes

    Kosher or sea salt

    Freshly ground pepper

1   medium Vidalia onion, finely chopped

6   cloves garlic, minced

2   medium carrots, thinly sliced

¼   cup/50 mL dry white wine

3   tbsp/45 mL brandy

2   tbsp/30 mL minced parsley

1   tsp/5 mL dried oregano

6   peppercorns

1   cup/250 mL drained, thinly sliced piquillo peppers or pimientos

4   oz/120 g small cremini mushrooms, brushed clean, stems trimmed, and caps quartered

2   tsp/10 mL tomato paste

Heat the oil in a large shallow flameproof casserole over medium-high heat, and brown the beef, sprinkling it with salt and pepper as it cooks. Add the onion and garlic to the casserole, and sauté until the onion has softened. Stir in the carrots, wine, brandy, parsley, oregano, and peppercorns. Bring to a boil over high heat. Cover and simmer for 1 hour.

Stir in the piquillo peppers, mushrooms, and tomato paste. Cover and simmer for 45–60 minutes until the beef is tender. Transfer the stew to a shallow serving dish. ▣

Estofado De Vaca Con Cebolletas De La Abuela

Beef Stew with Pearl Onions

Cinnamon and other eastern spices, like nutmeg and cloves, give an interesting twist to this fragrant Catalonian meal-in-a-pot, which is most likely of medieval origin.

Makes 4 servings

30	medium-size pearl onions (about ¾ lb/400 g)		1	tsp/5 mL dried oregano
2	lb/1 kg boneless stew beef, cut into ¾-inch/1.5 cm cubes		6	peppercorns
¼	cup/50 mL dry white wine		1	clove
3	tbsp/45 mL brandy		1	bay leaf
2	tbsp/30 mL minced parsley			Pinch of freshly grated nutmeg
2	tbsp/30 mL extra-virgin olive oil			Kosher or sea salt
2	cloves garlic, minced			Chicken broth as needed
1	1½-inch/3.5 cm cinnamon stick			

Bring a small saucepan of water to a boil, add the onions and boil for 3 minutes. Drain and rinse under cold water, then slip off their skins.

In a large pot, combine the onions, beef, wine, brandy, parsley, oil, garlic, cinnamon stick, oregano, peppercorns, clove, bay leaf, nutmeg, and salt to taste. Bring to a boil over high heat. Cover tightly and simmer for 2 hours until beef is tender, adding a little chicken broth if necessary to keep the stew from drying out and to provide enough sauce. Transfer the stew to a shallow serving dish. ▣

Huevos A La Flamenca

Baked Eggs with Chorizo and Vegetables

Without doubt, this is one of my favorite one-dish meals. It's so tasty and colorful made in individual earthenware casseroles, called *cazuelas*, and served piping hot straight from the oven.

Makes 2 servings

- 2 tbsp/30 mL extra-virgin olive oil
- 1 medium potato, peeled and cut into ½-inch/1 cm pieces
- 1 cup/250 mL finely chopped Vidalia onion
- 4 oz/120 g Serrano ham or prosciutto, finely chopped
- 6 tbsp/90 mL seeded and finely chopped green bell pepper (capsicum)
- 2 cloves garlic, minced
- 2 small tomatoes, chopped
- 2 tbsp/30 mL minced parsley
- ¼ tsp/1 mL sweet paprika, preferably Spanish smoked
- 4 oz/120 g sweet chorizo, thinly sliced
- ½ cup/125 mL chicken broth

- ¼ cup/50 mL cooked fresh or thawed frozen peas
- 2 tbsp/30 mL chopped pimiento
- Kosher or sea salt
- Freshly ground pepper
- 4 eggs
- 6 small asparagus spears, cooked
- Pimiento strips for garnish

Preheat the oven to 450°F/230°C. Heat the oil in a large skillet over medium heat. Scatter the potato pieces into the skillet, then cook, covered, until tender, turning occasionally. Remove the potato to a warm plate and set aside.

Add the onion, ham, green pepper, and garlic to the skillet and sauté until the onion is softened. Stir in the tomatoes, parsley, and paprika, and cook, stirring, for 2 minutes. Add the chorizo, chicken broth, peas, chopped pimiento, and salt and pepper to taste, and cook for a further 2 minutes. Stir in the potato.

Divide the onion mixture between 2 individual ovenproof casseroles, preferably Spanish earthenware cazuelas. Make 2 indentations in the onion mixture in each casserole. Break 1 egg into a cup and slide the egg into one of the indentations. Repeat with the remaining eggs. Sprinkle the eggs with salt and pepper to taste, then bake for about 8 minutes or until the eggs are just set (be careful not to overcook, since the eggs will continue to cook in the hot dishes after they are removed from the oven). Serve garnished with asparagus and pimiento. ▣

Estofado De Cerdo Al Estilo De Lagartera

Pork Stew with Potatoes

Lagartera is a small village in the province of Toledo famed for many centuries for its needlework. But the culinary competence of its women is another story. Young girls are taught to embroider, not to cook. Nevertheless, Lagarteranas do make some tasty dishes that require little effort. This pork stew is made with a minimum of ingredients, but the flavor is still exceptional because of the garlic and bay leaves it contains.

Makes 4 servings

- 2 tbsp/30 mL extra-virgin olive oil
- 1¾ lb/900 g boneless pork loin, cut into 1½-inch/3.5 cm cubes
  Kosher or sea salt
- 1 medium Vidalia onion, thinly sliced
- 3 cloves garlic, minced
- 2 bay leaves

- 1 medium tomato, finely chopped
- 1 cup/250 mL dry white wine
- ¼ cup/50 mL chicken broth
  Pinch of freshly grated nutmeg
  Freshly ground pepper
- 1 lb/500 g new or red waxy potatoes, scrubbed and cut into 1-inch/2.5 cm cubes

Heat the oil in a large shallow flameproof casserole over medium-high heat, and brown the pork, sprinkling it with salt as it cooks. Add the onion, garlic, and bay leaves to the casserole, and sauté until the onion has softened. Stir in the tomato and cook for 2 minutes. Add the wine, broth, nutmeg, and salt and pepper to taste. Bring to a boil over high heat. Cover and simmer for 25 minutes.

Add the potatoes. Cook, covered, for 20 minutes until the pork and potatoes are tender. Serve straight from the casserole. 🔲

Pastel De Carne Y Patatas

Spanish-Style Hash Casserole

I'm sure every country has its own version of hash, and Spain is no exception. A touch of brandy and nutmeg give the meat a unique flavor, and the egg, cheese, and crumb topping lend the casserole a most elegant final touch.

Makes 4–6 servings

2 lb/1 kg medium baking potatoes, peeled and cut into chunks	3 tbsp/45 mL minced parsley
2 cloves garlic, peeled	1 tsp/5 mL freshly grated nutmeg
¼ cup/50 mL extra-virgin olive oil	1 tsp/5 mL ground cumin
1 cup/250 mL warm milk	½ tsp/2 mL sweet paprika, preferably Spanish smoked
2 medium Vidalia onions, finely chopped	3 tbsp/45 mL dry breadcrumbs
8 oz/225 g ground beef	2 eggs
8 oz/225 g ground pork	Unsalted butter
8 oz/225 g ground veal	Grated Manchego or parmesan cheese
Kosher or sea salt	
Freshly ground pepper	
1 medium tomato, finely chopped	
¼ cup/50 mL brandy	

Combine the potatoes and garlic in a large saucepan with enough cold salted water to cover them. Bring to a boil over high heat. Reduce the heat to medium-low. Cover and simmer until tender. Drain well and return the potatoes and garlic to the saucepan. Add 2 tbsp/30 mL oil and most of the milk, then beat with an electric mixer until smooth, adding more milk as needed. Don't beat too much or the potatoes will become gluey. Set aside.

Preheat the oven to 350°F/180°C. Heat the remaining oil in a large skillet over medium heat, and sauté the onions for 2 minutes. Reduce the heat to low. Cover and cook for 10 minutes until the onion is softened. Increase the heat to high. Add the beef, pork, and veal, and season with salt and pepper, being generous with the pepper. Sauté the meat, breaking it up with the edge of a wooden spoon, until it loses its color. Add the tomato, brandy, parsley, nutmeg, cumin, and paprika, and sauté for about 5 minutes.

Oil a 12x8-inch (3 L) baking dish (preferably Pyrex) and sprinkle with half of the breadcrumbs. Spread a layer of potato in the bottom of the dish and top with a layer of meat. Repeat the layers until all the potato and meat are used up, ending with a layer of potato.

Beat the eggs with an electric mixer until thick, creamy, and lemon colored. Pour the eggs over the casserole. Dot with butter and sprinkle with the remaining breadcrumbs and grated cheese. Bake for about 30 minutes until golden brown. Loosen the edges and cut into portions, removing them from the dish with a metal pancake turner. ▣

Solomillo De Cerdo En Jarabe De Granada

Pork Tenderloin in Pomegranate Syrup

This recipe shows the influence of Andalucía's Moorish heritage in its sweet and savory combination. Any dish made with pomegranate is surely of Moorish descent (the symbol of the southern city of Granada is, in fact, the pomegranate, and the city's name derives from the fruit). Pork with fruit is, of course, a well-known match, and pork with pomegranate is one more example of that ideal pairing.

Makes 4 servings

1½ cups/375 mL unsweetened pomegranate juice	1 tbsp/15 mL minced fresh thyme leaves or ½ tsp/2 mL dried thyme
½ medium Vidalia onion, thinly sliced	2 bay leaves, crumbled
¼ cup/50 mL dry white wine	Kosher or sea salt
3 tbsp/45 mL extra-virgin olive oil	Freshly ground pepper
2 tbsp/30 mL minced parsley	2 pork tenderloins, about ¾–1 lb/375–500 g each
1 tbsp/15 mL minced fresh rosemary leaves or ½ tsp/2 mL dried rosemary	Chicken broth or water as needed

Put the pomegranate juice in a small saucepan and boil over high heat until juice has reduced by half. Remove from the heat and let cool completely.

In a deep bowl large enough to hold the tenderloins, stir together the pomegranate juice, onion, wine, oil, parsley, rosemary, thyme, bay leaves, and salt and pepper to taste. Add the tenderloins, turning to coat with the marinade. Cover and refrigerate for 2 hours, turning tenderloins occasionally.

Preheat the oven to 375°F/190°C. Remove the tenderloins from the marinade and put in a shallow roasting pan. Scatter the onion from the marinade around them and add just enough of the marinade to moisten the pan, reserving the remainder. Roast the tenderloins, uncovered, for 30–40 minutes, until a meat thermometer registers 145°F/63°C, adding more marinade occasionally to keep the pan juices from burning. By the time the meat is done, you should have added all the marinade; if more liquid is needed, add a little chicken broth or water.

Transfer the tenderloins to a cutting board, tent loosely with foil and let rest for 10 minutes. Cut the tenderloins at an angle into ½-inch/1 cm slices and arrange on a platter. Drizzle with the juices from the roasting pan. 🗗

Solomillo De Cerdo Con Cebolla Estofada

Pork Tenderloin with Stewed Onions

This flavorful pork tenderloin, with a hint of mustard and an abundance of sweet, slow-cooked onions, is one of my favorites. If you make the onions in advance, the tenderloins will cook in about 35 minutes. You can serve the meat with the mustard dipping sauce, but the dish is also excellent on its own.

Makes 4 servings

2 pork tenderloins, about ¾–1 lb/375–500 g each	¼ tsp/1 mL dried thyme
Kosher or sea salt	1 bay leaf
Freshly ground pepper	1 tbsp/15 mL granulated sugar
2 tbsp/30 mL grainy mustard	8 peppercorns
2 tbsp/30 mL extra-virgin olive oil	Chicken broth as needed
4 medium Vidalia onions, thinly sliced	¼ cup/50 mL mustard powder (optional)
2 cloves garlic, minced	

Sprinkle the tenderloins with salt and pepper, patting the meat so that the salt and pepper adhere. Brush on all sides with the grainy mustard.

Heat the oil in a large shallow flameproof casserole over medium-high heat, and sauté the tenderloins until well browned on all sides (they will not be cooked through). Remove to a plate and refrigerate until needed.

Add the onions, garlic, thyme, and bay leaf to the casserole and sauté until onions are slightly softened. Reduce the heat to low. Cook, uncovered, for 1 hour, stirring occasionally, until onions are very soft. Stir in the sugar and peppercorns. Cook, covered, for 1 hour, stirring occasionally and adding a little chicken broth if the onions look too dry.

Return the tenderloins to the casserole. Cover and cook for about 35 minutes, or until a meat thermometer inserted into the thickest part of the tenderloins registers 145°F/63°C.

Remove the tenderloins to a board and cut the meant diagonally into ¼-inch/3 mm slices. If there doesn't seem to be enough sauce, add a little more chicken broth to the onions. Arrange the pork on a platter and spoon the onions and sauce over the meat. Stir 3 tbsp/45 mL cold water into the mustard powder in a small bowl and serve, if you wish, with the pork. ▣

Albóndigas En Salsa De Limón

Meatballs in Lemon Sauce

These pork and veal meatballs are cooked in a tasty egg yolk, lemon, and saffron sauce that's quite unlike any other Spanish sauce I know. Serve with very small boiled new potatoes.

Makes 4 servings

For meatballs:

- 6 tbsp/90 mL dry breadcrumbs
- ¼ cup/50 mL milk
- ¾ lb/400 g ground veal
- ¾ lb/400 g ground pork
- 2 eggs
- 3 tbsp/45 mL freshly squeezed lemon juice
- 2 tbsp/30 mL minced parsley
- 2 tbsp/30 mL finely chopped Serrano ham or prosciutto
- 1½ tbsp/22 mL minced fresh thyme leaves or ¾ tsp/3 mL dried thyme
- 2 cloves garlic, minced
- 1½ tsp/7 mL kosher or sea salt
- ½ tsp/2 mL freshly ground pepper
- All-purpose flour for dusting

For sauce:

- 2 tbsp/30 mL extra-virgin olive oil
- ¼ cup/50 mL finely chopped Vidalia onion
- ¾ cup/175 mL chicken broth
- 3 tbsp/45 mL dry white wine
- 3 tbsp/45 mL minced parsley
- 1 clove garlic, minced
- Pinch of crumbled saffron threads
- Kosher or sea salt
- 4 oz/120 g mushrooms, brushed clean, stems trimmed, and caps halved or quartered
- 2 tbsp/30 mL freshly squeezed lemon juice
- 2 egg yolks
- Chicken broth or water as needed

To prepare the meatballs, combine the breadcrumbs with the milk in a large bowl. Gently mix in the ground veal and pork, eggs, lemon juice, parsley, ham, thyme, garlic, salt, and pepper. Shape into 1½- inch/3.5 cm meatballs and dust with flour.

To prepare the sauce, heat the oil in a shallow flameproof casserole over medium-high heat, and sauté the meatballs until brown on all sides. Add the onion and sauté until softened. Stir in the broth and wine. Bring to a boil over high heat. Cover and simmer for 40 minutes.

Mash 2 tbsp/30 mL parsley, the garlic, saffron, and a pinch of salt to a paste in a mortar, or process in a mini food processor until finely minced.

Remove the meatballs to a warm plate and keep warm. Strain the sauce through a fine sieve, pressing on the solids with the back of a metal soup ladle to extract as much liquid as possible. Return the sauce to the casserole and add the mushrooms, mortar mixture, and lemon juice.

Whisk the egg yolks with a little of the hot sauce from the casserole in a small bowl, then add back to the casserole. Cook over low heat, stirring constantly, until thickened (do not boil). If the sauce seems too thick, add a little broth or water. Return the meatballs to the sauce and simmer for 1 minute. Serve straight from the casserole, sprinkled with the remaining parsley. ◫

Caldereta De Cordero

Lamb Stew with New Potatoes

This recipe has ingredients common to Spain, but the taste is special because of the dried red pepper (*ñora*), which gives depth of flavor to the stew.

Makes 4 servings

3 tbsp/45 mL extra-virgin olive oil	Freshly ground pepper
2 small dried sweet red peppers (*ñoras*), or 1 dried New Mexico chile, seeds and stems removed	¼ cup/50 mL brandy
	½ tsp/2 mL dried thyme
1 medium Vidalia onion, finely chopped	1 bay leaf
6 cloves garlic, peeled	¾ lb/375 g very small (1½-inch/3.5 cm diameter) new potatoes, scrubbed
2–2 ½ lb/1–1.2 kg boneless leg of lamb, cut into 1½-inch/3.5 cm pieces	¾ cup/175 mL chicken broth
Kosher or sea salt	⅓ cup/75 mL dry white wine

Heat the oil in a large pot over medium heat and sauté the dried peppers, onion, and garlic for 2 minutes. Reduce the heat to medium-low. Add the lamb, sprinkle with salt and pepper, and sauté until the meat loses its color. Add the brandy, thyme, and bay leaf. Bring to a boil over high heat. Cover and simmer for 30 minutes.

Remove the dried peppers and garlic cloves from the pot and mash to a paste in a mortar. Return the mortar mixture to the pot. Add the potatoes, broth, and wine. Bring to a boil over high heat. Cover and simmer for 30 minutes until the potatoes and lamb are tender. Transfer the stew to a shallow serving dish. ▣

Cordero Mozárabe
Moorish Lamb Stew

In Cazalla de la Sierra in the mountains of the province of Sevilla, Julia Piñedo and her sister love to serve dishes from their town's Moorish past in their restaurant Posada del Moro. One of their favorite recipes is this wonderful lamb stew with its Moorish touches of spice—cinnamon, nutmeg, and ginger—and dried fruits, such as apricots, figs, and raisins.

Makes 4 servings

2 tbsp/30 mL extra-virgin olive oil	½ tsp/2 mL ground coriander
2 lb/1 kg boneless lamb shoulder, cut into 1½-inch/3.5 cm pieces	6 peppercorns
Kosher or sea salt	1 bay leaf
Freshly ground pepper	Pinch of cinnamon
1 medium Vidalia onion, chopped	Pinch of grated nutmeg
1 cup/250 mL dry red wine	Kosher or sea salt
¼ cup/50 mL chicken broth	8 dried apricots
2 tbsp/30 mL brandy	6 dried figs, thinly sliced crosswise
½ tsp/2 mL peeled and minced fresh ginger	2 tbsp/30 mL raisins

Heat the oil in a large pot over medium-high heat, and brown the lamb, sprinkling it with salt and pepper as it cooks. Add the onion and sauté until the onion is softened. Stir in the wine, broth, brandy, ginger, coriander, peppercorns, bay leaf, cinnamon, nutmeg, and salt to taste. Bring to a boil over high heat. Cover and simmer for 1 hour until lamb is tender.

With a slotted spoon, remove lamb to a serving platter and keep warm. Increase heat to high and boil contents of the pot until the sauce has reduced and thickened slightly. Strain through a fine sieve, pressing on the solids with the back of a metal soup ladle to extract as much liquid as possible. Return the sauce to the pot, and add the apricots, figs, and raisins. Bring to a boil. Cover and simmer for 10 minutes. Pour the sauce over the lamb.

Rabo De Toro

Oxtail Stew with Juniper Berries

Although Andalucía, where bulls are typically bred, usually takes credit for oxtail stew—rich, fork-tender meat in a wonderful sauce—this version, scented with juniper berries, comes from the region of Aragón. Ask your butcher to cut the oxtail into pieces.

Makes 4 servings

2	tbsp/30 mL extra-virgin olive oil
3½–4	lb/1.7–2 kg oxtail, cut crosswise into 2-inch/5 cm pieces
1	medium Vidalia onion, chopped
1	medium carrot, thickly sliced
1½	tsp/7 mL dried oregano
1½	tsp/7 mL minced fresh thyme leaves or ¼ tsp/1 mL dried thyme

6	peppercorns
5	dried juniper berries
¼	tsp/1 mL sweet paprika, preferably Spanish smoked
	Kosher or sea salt
1	small tomato, chopped
2	cups/500 mL dry white wine

Heat the oil in a large deep flameproof casserole over medium-high heat. Add the oxtail, onion, carrot, oregano, thyme, peppercorns, juniper berries, paprika, and salt to taste. Cook, stirring often, until the oxtail is lightly browned and the onion is softened.

Add the tomato and cook for 2–3 minutes, then add the wine. Bring to a boil over high heat. Reduce the heat to medium-low. Simmer, uncovered, for about 3 hours or until most of the liquid has evaporated and the oxtail is very tender. If the liquid evaporates too quickly, cover the casserole and continue cooking until the oxtail is very tender. Serve straight from the casserole. ▣

Vegetables and Legumes

Patatas Al Azafrán

Sautéed Saffron-Scented Potatoes

Saffron gives a golden gleam to the onion that garnishes the potatoes in this popular dish from Spain's northern Basque Country. These potatoes are meant to complement simple meat, fish, poultry, and game dishes.

Makes 4 servings

5 tbsp/75 mL extra-virgin olive oil	¼ tsp/1 mL crumbled saffron threads
1 medium Vidalia onion, thinly sliced	4 medium baking potatoes, peeled and thinly sliced
1 bay leaf	Kosher or sea salt
2 tbsp/30 mL chicken broth	
2 tbsp/30 mL dry white wine	2 tbsp/30 mL minced parsley

Heat 2 tbsp/30 mL oil in a large skillet over medium heat. Add the onion and bay leaf, and sauté gently for about 10 minutes until softened. Stir in the chicken broth, wine, and saffron, and cook for 1 minute to evaporate some of the liquid. Remove the onion mixture to a plate and discard the bay leaf.

Wipe out the skillet and heat the remaining oil over medium-high heat. Add the potato slices one at a time, so they don't stick together. Sprinkle with salt to taste. Turn the potato slices over and reduce the heat to low. Cook, covered, for about 20 minutes until potatoes are tender, lifting and turning them occasionally. Arrange the potatoes on a platter and spoon the onions over the top. Serve sprinkled with parsley. ◐

Patatas Al Jerez

Sherry-Infused Baked Sliced Potatoes

I ate these potatoes one day at the Restaurante Bigote in the southern Spanish town of Sanlúcar de Barrameda, and they really captured my attention. They seemed simple and perfectly straightforward, but there was something extraordinary about them that I could not identify. It turned out to be the exquisite flavor of *manzanilla*, the bone-dry sherry made in this town, and the special ingredient in so much local cooking.

Makes 4 servings

¼ cup/50 mL extra-virgin olive oil	¼ medium Vidalia onion, thinly sliced
1½ lb/750 g white potatoes, peeled and thinly sliced	2 bay leaves, torn in half
Kosher or sea salt	3 tbsp/45 mL very dry sherry, such as *manzanilla*
Freshly ground pepper	2 tbsp/30 mL minced parsley

Preheat the oven to 300°F/150°C. Grease a 12x8-inch (3 L) baking dish (preferably nonstick or Pyrex) with ½ tbsp/7 mL oil. Arrange half of the potatoes in a slightly overlapping layer in the bottom of the dish, and sprinkle with salt and pepper. Scatter the onion and bay leaves over the potatoes. Arrange the remaining potatoes over the onion, sprinkling again with salt and pepper. Drizzle the remaining oil over the potatoes. Bake, uncovered, for 30 minutes. Turn the potatoes with a spatula. Cover the dish loosely with foil and cook for 20 minutes until the potatoes are almost tender.

Increase the oven temperature to 450°F/230°C. Sprinkle the sherry over the potatoes. Cover again loosely with foil, and bake until the sherry is absorbed and the potatoes are tender, about 10 minutes. Sprinkle with parsley before serving. ◓

Patatas Guisadas Con Costillas De Cerdo

Stewed Potatoes Rioja-Style with Pork Ribs

On a trip to the Toro wine region in western Castile, I visited Bodegas Fariña and lunched at the winery on humble Castilian fare, including this exceptional potato stew. Spanish bittersweet smoked paprika is the key ingredient that transforms an otherwise ordinary dish into something quite extraordinary.

The pork ribs need to be in small pieces, and it's best to leave that job to your butcher. The recipe calls for breaking the potatoes with the point of a knife into irregular pieces, a technique that really makes a difference to the texture and taste.

Makes 4 servings

1 small Vidalia onion, coarsely chopped	1¾ lb/900 g baby back pork ribs, sawed lengthwise into 1½-inch/3.5 cm strips, then each strip cut into 2-rib pieces
4 cloves garlic, minced	3 tbsp/45 mL extra-virgin olive oil
3 tbsp/45 mL minced parsley	1½ cups/375 mL dry white wine
2 tsp/10 mL paprika, preferably Spanish smoked bittersweet	3½ lb/1.7 kg baking potatoes, peeled
¾ tsp/3 mL ground cumin	1 small tomato, diced
½ tsp/2 mL dried oregano	
1 large bay leaf	
Pinch of hot paprika, preferably Spanish smoked or cayenne	
Kosher or sea salt	
Freshly ground pepper	

Combine the onion, garlic, parsley, 1¼ tsp/6 mL bittersweet paprika, cumin, oregano, bay leaf, hot paprika, and salt and pepper to taste in a large bowl. Add the ribs, turning to coat them well with the spices. Cover and marinate for 1 hour at room temperature, or several hours (or overnight) in the refrigerator.

Heat the oil in a large shallow casserole over medium heat. Add the ribs with their marinade and sauté, turning once, until the meat loses its color. Pour in 3 cups/750 mL water and the wine. Bring to a boil over high heat. Cover and simmer for 1½ hours until meat is tender.

Break the potatoes into irregular, 1½–2-inch/3.5–5 cm pieces by inserting the point of a sturdy, sharp paring knife into the potatoes, then twisting the knife until the pieces of potato break off. Add the potato pieces to the casserole, along with the tomato, remaining bittersweet paprika, and more hot paprika, cumin, and salt to taste. Cover and cook for 15 minutes until the potatoes are just tender. Serve in shallow soup bowls with plenty of good crusty bread. ◔

Patatas Viudas

"Widowed" Potatoes

This simple potato preparation really has no other ingredients save the potatoes and a touch of garlic and onion, thus the name "widowed" potatoes. It is favored by Castilian convent nuns as a tasty, simple, and most frugal meal.

Makes 4 servings

4 medium potatoes, peeled and thinly sliced	2 tbsp/30 mL minced parsley
Kosher or sea salt	1 bay leaf
2 tbsp/30 mL extra-virgin olive oil	½ tsp/2 mL sweet or hot paprika, preferably Spanish smoked
¾ cup/175 mL finely chopped Vidalia onion	
2 cloves garlic, minced	

Put the potatoes in a large saucepan with enough cold salted water to cover them. Bring to a boil over high heat. Reduce the heat to medium-low. Cover and simmer until just tender. Drain well, reserving ¼ cup/50 mL cooking liquid.

Meanwhile, heat the oil in a large skillet over medium heat, and sauté the onion, garlic, parsley, and bay leaf for about 2 minutes. Reduce the heat to low. Cover and cook gently until the onions are softened, about 10 minutes. Stir in the paprika.

Add the potatoes and reserved cooking liquid to the skillet and cook, stirring gently, for 2 to 3 minutes until combined and heated through. Transfer to a serving platter. ◐

Alubias Rojas De Goierri

Basque Red Bean Stew

This exceptional dish of red beans with chorizo and blood sausage comes from the mother of famed Basque chef Juan Mari Arzak, who created "New Basque Cuisine." Because the meats are pre-cooked, the fat is greatly reduced. Bean stews in the Basque Country are typically accompanied by sautéed cabbage and the long, skinny hot Basque peppers packed in vinegar, called *guindillas vascas*.

Makes 4 servings

For beans:

- 2 cups/500 mL dried deep red beans, preferably Spanish
- 1 medium Vidalia onion, cut in half
- 1 large carrot, cut in half crosswise
- 1 small leek (white part only)
- ¼ cup/50 mL extra-virgin olive oil
  Kosher or sea salt
- 4 oz/120 g sweet semi-cured chorizo
- 4 oz/120 g *morcilla* (Spanish blood sausage)
- 1 4-oz/120 g piece slab bacon
- 2 medium green bell peppers (capsicums), seeded and finely chopped
- 3 cloves garlic, minced
- 2 tsp/10 mL sweet paprika, preferably Spanish smoked

For sautéed cabbage:

- 3 tbsp/45 mL extra-virgin olive oil
- ¼ cup/50 mL finely chopped Vidalia onion
- 2 cloves garlic, minced
- 1 small cabbage, cored and coarsely chopped
  Kosher or sea salt
  Freshly ground pepper
  Guindillas vascas to serve (see note above)

To prepare the beans, soak them overnight in enough cold water to cover them. Drain, then combine in a large pot with 6 cups/1.5 L water, half the onion, the carrot, leek, 2 tbsp/30 mL oil, and salt to taste. Bring to a boil over high heat. Cover and simmer for about 2 hours until the beans are tender. Drain, discarding the onion, carrot, and leek. Put beans in a large serving dish and keep warm.

Meanwhile, prick the chorizo and *morcilla* with a fork, and put in a large skillet with the slab bacon. Add enough water to cover the meats. Bring to a boil over high heat. Simmer, uncovered, for 20 minutes until the sausages are cooked through. Cut the sausages and bacon into 1-inch/2.5 cm pieces and keep warm. Wipe out the skillet.

Finely chop the remaining onion half. Heat the remaining oil in the skillet over medium heat and sauté the onion, green pepper, and garlic for 10 minutes. Cover and cook for 15 minutes until onion is very soft. Add the onion mixture, sausages, and bacon to the beans. Season with salt to taste and keep warm.

To prepare the sautéed cabbage, heat the oil in a large skillet over medium heat and sauté the onion and garlic until the onion is softened. Add the cabbage and salt and pepper to taste and sauté for about 10 minutes until the cabbage is tender-crisp. Cover and cook until tender.

Serve the beans with the sautéed cabbage and *guindillas vascas*. ◗

Berenjena Rebozada A La Morisca

Moorish-Style Battered Eggplant

Eggplant, as old as civilization itself, was introduced to Spain from the Far East by the Moors, who favored it in their cooking. It continued to be an important ingredient in medieval times and appears in the 16th century cookbook of chef Ruperto de Nola, seasoned with such Moorish flavors as ginger, coriander, cloves, and nutmeg. In this batter-fried preparation it's the Moorish touch of crushed coriander seed that brings the mild-flavored eggplant to life.

Makes 4 servings

For eggplant:

1 1½-lb/750 g eggplant, peeled and thinly sliced crosswise

   Kosher or sea salt

1 egg

¼ cup/50 mL dry white wine

1 cup/250 mL all-purpose flour

½ cup/125 mL seltzer (soda) water

1 tbsp/15 mL minced cilantro

1½ tsp/7 mL crushed coriander seeds

1 clove garlic, minced

   Freshly ground pepper

   Olive oil for frying

For garnish:

1 tbsp/15 mL minced cilantro

   Crushed coriander seed to taste

2 tbsp/30 mL liquid honey

To prepare the eggplant, arrange the eggplant slices in layers in a colander, salting each layer well. Let stand for 15 minutes, then rinse and drain. Dry well on paper towels.

Whisk together the egg and wine in a medium bowl. Stir in the flour, seltzer water, cilantro, coriander, garlic, and salt and pepper to taste.

Pour the oil into a large skillet to a depth of 1½ inches/3.5 cm (or better still, use a deep-fryer) and heat over high heat until the oil quickly browns a cube of bread. Dip the eggplant slices in the batter and drop a few at a time into the hot oil. (If the batter becomes too thick, thin it with a little water until it's the consistency of a thick pancake batter.) Fry, in batches, until the eggplant slices are cooked and golden, turning once. Drain on paper towels, sprinkle with the cilantro and crushed coriander seed, and drizzle with the honey. Serve at once. ◐

Acelgas Salteadas Con Migas
Sautéed Swiss Chard with Bread Bits and Cumin

Swiss chard, so rich in nutrients, is without doubt a favorite green in Spain, especially when sautéed with garlic and crunchy bread cubes.

Makes 4 servings

Kosher or sea salt

1–1½ lb/500–750 g washed and trimmed Swiss chard

3 tbsp/45 mL extra-virgin olive oil

¼ cup/50 mL minced Vidalia onion

2 cloves garlic, minced

2 slices firm-textured, French-style bread, cut into cubes

1 tsp/5 mL red wine vinegar

½ tsp/2 mL paprika, preferably Spanish smoked bittersweet

¼ tsp/1 mL ground cumin

Bring a large pot of salted water to a boil. Add the Swiss chard and 1 tbsp/15 mL oil, and simmer for about 12 minutes until tender. Drain well in a colander, then chop the Swiss chard coarsely.

Heat the remaining oil in a large skillet over medium heat, and sauté the onion and garlic until the onion is softened. Add the bread cubes, and sauté until golden on all sides. Stir in the vinegar, paprika, and cumin, and sauté for 1–2 minutes. Stir in the Swiss chard. Transfer to a serving platter. ◖

Judías Verdes Salteadas Con Jamón Y Huevos Duros

Sautéed Green Beans with Ham, Pimientos, and Hard-Cooked Eggs

Vegetables in Spain are more likely to be first courses than side dishes, and that's why you will find additions like hard-cooked egg, as in this recipe, to add interest and flavor.

Makes 4 servings

Kosher or sea salt	¼ tsp/1 mL sweet paprika, preferably Spanish smoked
1½ lb/750 g broad flat green beans, trimmed	2 tbsp/30 mL minced parsley
2 tbsp/30 mL extra-virgin olive oil	¼ tsp/1 mL crushed hot red chile flakes
1 clove garlic, peeled and lightly crushed	2 hard-cooked eggs, cut into quarters
½ cup/125 mL chopped Serrano ham or prosciutto	1 drained piquillo pepper, cut into thin strips
2 tsp/10 mL red wine vinegar	

Bring a large pot of salted water to a boil over high heat, add the beans and cook for about 20 minutes until tender. Drain.

Heat the oil and garlic in a large skillet over medium heat. Add the beans and ham, and sauté until ham is lightly browned. Reduce the heat to low. Stir in the vinegar and paprika, and sauté for 1 minute. Transfer to a serving platter. Sprinkle with the parsley and chile flakes, and serve garnished with the eggs and piquillo pepper. ◗

Espinacas Con Membrillo Y Piñones

Spinach Sautéed with Quince and Toasted Pine Nuts

El Rebost de la Cartoixa is a restaurant in the Catalan hamlet of Scala Dei, in the region of El Priorat, renowned for its fine wines. The simple food at the restaurant, such as this spinach, given a touch of sweetness from the quince—so very Catalan—was wonderful.

In Spain spinach and other greens are often served in combination with fruit and nuts, creating a wonderful blend of flavors and textures. Quince, a fruit related to the apple, is an ideal match for spinach, and the pine nuts add a final touch.

Makes 4 servings

2 tbsp/30 mL extra-virgin olive oil	½ tsp/2 mL sweet paprika, preferably Spanish smoked
1 quince (about ½ lb/250 g) or large Golden Delicious apple, cored, peeled, and cut into ½-inch/1 cm cubes	15 cups/3.7 L baby spinach, well washed and stems trimmed
1 medium Vidalia onion, finely chopped	Kosher or sea salt
1 clove garlic, peeled and lightly crushed	Freshly ground pepper
2 tbsp/30 mL pine nuts	

Heat the oil in a large deep skillet over medium heat, and sauté the quince, onion, and garlic for 2 minutes. Reduce the heat to low. Cover and cook for 10 minutes. Discard the garlic.

Add the pine nuts and paprika to the skillet, and sauté until the nuts are lightly golden. Gradually add the spinach, letting the leaves wilt slightly before adding more. Season with salt and pepper to taste, and sauté for 1 minute. Cover and cook for about 3 minutes until spinach has wilted and is tender. Transfer to a serving platter. ◐

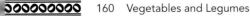

Judías Blancas Rehogadas

Sautéed White Beans

In Spain beans are usually part of a stew with chorizo and ham. But here they are prepared in Catalan style—sautéed with garlic and a touch of saffron and anchovy—and served on their own.

Makes 4 servings

1⅓	cups/325 mL small dried white beans		2	tbsp/30 mL extra-virgin olive oil
1	small Vidalia onion		1	drained and chopped piquillo pepper
½	whole head garlic, loose skin removed		2	anchovy fillets, chopped
2	sprigs parsley		¼	tsp/1 mL dried thyme
1	bay leaf		¼	tsp/1 mL sweet paprika, preferably Spanish smoked
	Pinch of crumbled saffron threads		¼	tsp/1 mL ground cumin
	Kosher or sea salt			
	Freshly ground pepper			

Soak the beans overnight in enough cold water to cover them. Drain, then combine in a large pot with 6 cups/1.5 L water, the onion, whole garlic head, parsley, bay leaf, saffron, and salt and pepper to taste. Bring to a boil over high heat. Cover and simmer for about 2 hours until the beans are tender. Drain the beans, reserving the garlic but discarding the onion, parsley, and bay leaf. Squeeze the garlic flesh into the beans, discarding the skin.

Heat the oil in a large skillet over high heat. Add the beans and sauté, stirring often, until the beans are slightly crunchy. Stir in the piquillo pepper, anchovies, thyme, paprika, cumin, and salt and pepper to taste. Transfer to a serving platter. ◓

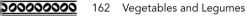

Fabes Con Almejas

Beans with Clams

The combination of beans and clams, a specialty of the region of Asturias, may sound unlikely, but you will be surprised how beautifully these tastes blend and how very delicious this dish is.

Makes 4–6 servings

For beans:

- 2 cups/500 mL large white dried beans
- 1 Vidalia onion, cut in half
- 1 carrot, cut in half crosswise
- 1 green bell pepper (capsicum), seeded and finely chopped
- 8 cloves garlic, peeled
- 2 sprigs parsley
- 2 bay leaves
  - Kosher or sea salt

For clams:

- 6 tbsp/90 mL extra-virgin olive oil
- 2 tbsp/30 mL minced Vidalia onion
- 4 cloves garlic, minced
- 1 tbsp/15 mL sweet paprika, preferably Spanish smoked
- ½ cup/125 mL dry white wine
- 2 tbsp/30 mL minced parsley
- ½ dried red chile pepper (such as Spanish *guindilla* or *guajillo*), crumbled and seeds removed
- 36 Manila clams
  - Pinch of crumbled saffron threads
  - Kosher or sea salt
  - Freshly ground pepper

To prepare the beans, soak them overnight in cold water to cover. Drain, then combine in a large pot with 6 cups/1.5 L water, the onion, carrot, green pepper, garlic, parsley sprigs, bay leaves, and salt to taste. Bring to a boil over high heat. Cover and simmer for about 2 hours or until beans are tender. Discard the onion, carrot, garlic, parsley, and bay leaves. Transfer the beans, green pepper, and their cooking liquid to a serving dish, and keep warm.

To prepare the clams, heat the oil in a large skillet over medium heat, and sauté the onion and garlic until the onion is softened. Sprinkle in the paprika and stir well. Stir in the wine, parsley, and chile pepper. Bring to a boil. Add the clams and cook for 4–6 minutes or until the clams open, discarding any clams that remain closed. Add the clam mixture to the beans, along with the saffron, and salt and pepper to taste. Serve in wide bowls. ◐

Tortilla Española De Patata

Spanish Potato Omelet

This simple omelet is a favorite Sunday night meal in our house. I like to serve it at room temperature with sausages and piquillo peppers.

Makes 4–6 servings

- 1 cup/250 mL extra-virgin olive oil
- 4 large baking potatoes, peeled and cut crosswise into ⅛-inch/3 mm slices

    Kosher or sea salt

- 1 large Vidalia onion, thinly sliced
- 4 eggs

Heat the oil in an 8- or 9-inch (20 or 23 cm) skillet over medium heat. Arrange a layer of potato slices in the skillet, adding them one at a time so they don't stick together. Sprinkle potatoes lightly with salt. Arrange a layer of onion over the potato, sprinkling lightly with salt. Repeat layers, sprinkling each lightly with salt, until all potatoes and onion are used up. Cook, lifting and turning the potatoes occasionally, until they are tender but not brown. Drain the potato mixture in a colander, reserving about 3 tbsp/45 mL of the oil. Wipe out the skillet, scraping off any stuck-on pieces.

In a large bowl, beat the eggs lightly with a fork. Season with salt to taste. Add the potato mixture, pressing down on the potatoes with an egg lifter to ensure they're well coated with egg. Let stand for 15 minutes.

Heat 2 tbsp/30 mL of the reserved oil in the same skillet over high heat until it smokes. Add the egg-potato mixture, spreading it out quickly with an egg lifter to cover the base of the skillet. Reduce the heat to medium-high and cook, shaking the skillet often to prevent the omelet from sticking. When the eggs are starting to brown underneath, invert a large plate over the skillet. Wearing oven mitts, invert skillet and plate together to flip the omelet onto the plate. Add the remaining 1 tbsp/15 mL oil to the skillet, then slide the omelet back into the skillet and cook until the underside is browned.

Reduce the heat to medium and cook for 3 to 5 minutes, flipping the omelet two or three more times until golden brown on the outside but still moist in the center. Slide the omelet onto a serving plate and let cool to room temperature. Serve cut into wedges. ◓

POSTRES

Desserts

Arroz Con Leche Al Estilo Asturiano

Rice Pudding Asturian Style

This creamy and seemingly rich rice pudding has, in fact, no eggs or cream, and is the purest-tasting rice pudding I have ever eaten. Be sure your milk is absolutely fresh and the rice short-grain.

Makes 8 servings

¾ cup/175 mL Valencian short-grain or Arborio rice

8 cups/2 L whole milk

Grated zest of ½ lemon

1 3-inch/8 cm cinnamon stick

Pinch of kosher or sea salt

⅔ cup/150 mL granulated sugar

1 tbsp/15 mL brandy

Cinnamon for garnish

Rinse the rice in a sieve and drain well. Combine the rice with the milk, lemon zest, cinnamon stick, and salt in a large saucepan. Bring to a boil over high heat. Simmer very gently, uncovered, for 3 hours, stirring often, until the pudding has the consistency of a soft custard (it will continue to thicken as it cools). Stir in the sugar, and simmer for 15 minutes.

Remove from the heat and let cool slightly, stirring occasionally. Discard the cinnamon stick and stir in the brandy. Spoon the pudding into 8 shallow dessert bowls, preferably flat-bottomed earthenware bowls. Refrigerate until cold. Let the puddings stand at room temperature for about 1 hour before serving. Sprinkle tops with cinnamon. ∿

Crema Catalana

Catalan Cream

Catalan custard—an enriched soft custard covered with a crackling caramelized sugar coating—has traveled the world, and is as likely to show up in New York as in Barcelona. A blowtorch greatly simplifies making the sugar topping.

Makes 6 servings

2	tbsp plus ½ tsp/32 mL cornstarch
2¾	cups/675 mL whole milk
6	egg yolks
½	lemon
½	cup/125 mL granulated sugar
1	3-inch/8 cm cinnamon stick

For topping:

⅓ cup/75 mL granulated sugar

Stir together the cornstarch and 2 tbsp/30 mL milk in a medium bowl until smooth. Stir in the egg yolks and set aside.

With a sharp knife, pare the rind from the lemon, avoiding the white pith. Stir together the lemon rind, remaining milk, the sugar, and cinnamon stick in a medium saucepan. Bring to a boil over medium-high heat. Simmer, uncovered, for 15 minutes. Gradually whisk the hot milk into the cornstarch mixture. Return the custard to the saucepan and cook over medium heat, stirring constantly, until it starts to bubble. Discard the lemon rind and cinnamon stick. Spoon the custard into 6 shallow dessert bowls, preferably flat-bottomed earthenware bowls. Let cool without stirring.

To prepare the topping, sprinkle 1 tbsp/15 mL sugar evenly over each pudding. Ignite a blowtorch and caramelize the sugar until evenly melted, moving the torch constantly so that the sugar doesn't burn. Serve at once. ∽

Hojaldre De Manzana

Spiced Stewed Apples in Puff Pastry

Apples appeared in Spain during Roman rule and found their ideal climate in the north of the country. Spanish reineta apples are similar to our Golden Delicious, which I have used in this first-rate dessert.

Makes 4 servings

6 oz/170 g homemade or good-quality purchased puff pastry

½ lemon

1 cup/250 mL dry white wine

⅔ cup/150 mL granulated sugar

1 3-inch/8 cm cinnamon stick

5 cloves

¼ tsp/1 mL ground cardamom

¼ tsp/1 mL freshly grated nutmeg

2 large Golden Delicious apples

Melted vanilla ice cream or lightly sweetened heavy (whipping) cream

Confectioners' (icing) sugar for dusting

Preheat the oven to 400°F/200°C. Roll out the puff pastry to ⅛ inch/3 mm thickness, then cut into four 4x3-inch/10x8 cm rectangles. Prick the rectangles all over with a fork, then arrange a little apart on a large ungreased baking sheet. Bake for 8 to 10 minutes until puffed and golden brown. Turn off the oven, open the door slightly, and leave the pastries in the oven for about 5 minutes to crisp them further.

With a sharp knife, pare the rind from the lemon, avoiding the white pith. Stir together the lemon rind, wine, sugar, cinnamon stick, cloves, cardamom, and nutmeg in a medium saucepan. Bring to a boil over high heat. Simmer for about 10 minutes, stirring occasionally.

Meanwhile, peel, quarter, and core the apples. Cut each quarter into ¼-inch/5 mm wedges, then cut each wedge crosswise into ¾-inch/1.5 cm pieces. Add the apples to the saucepan and cook for 30 minutes until the apples are very tender.

With a slotted spoon, remove the apples to a bowl. Simmer the syrup until it has thickened and is slightly caramelized. Remove the saucepan from the heat. Return the apples to the saucepan and let cool completely. Discard the lemon rind, cinnamon stick, and cloves.

Split each pastry in half horizontally. Spoon about 2 tbsp/30 mL stewed apples on the bottom half of each pastry, then replace top halves. Serve each pastry on a pool of melted ice cream or sweetened heavy cream. Dust tops with confectioners' sugar. ↶

Yoghurt Con Manzana Y Grosellas
Whole Milk Yogurt with Apples and Red Berries

I discovered this pleasing but extremely simple dessert in a bed-and-breakfast in the tiny town of Valverde de los Arroyos in the province of Guadalajara. It is important to use rich whole milk yogurt, preferably Greek.

Makes 4 servings

- 2   cups/500 mL Greek-style whole milk yogurt
- 2   Golden Delicious apples, peeled, cored, and coarsely grated
- 1   tsp/5 mL sesame seeds
- 3   tbsp/45 mL liquid honey

    Red berries, such as red currants, small strawberries, and/or raspberries for garnish

Divide the yogurt among 4 individual dessert bowls and sprinkle evenly with the apple and sesame seeds. Drizzle each portion with honey and garnish with the berries. ⟿

Flan Con Azúcar Acaramelado

Caramel Custard

Baked custard with caramelized sugar, commonly known in Spain as *flan*, is light and refreshing, and celebrated the world over. It's a delightful way to end a meal, and couldn't be simpler to make. A sprinkling of coconut on top makes for a sweet finish.

Makes 6 servings

For caramelized sugar syrup:

½ cup/125 mL granulated sugar

7 tbsp/105 mL hot water

For flan:

3 eggs

3 egg yolks

2½ cups/625 mL whole milk

6 tbsp/90 mL granulated sugar

¼ tsp/1 mL grated lemon zest

To prepare the caramelized sugar syrup, stir together the sugar and 3 tbsp/45 mL water in a small saucepan. Bring to a boil over high heat. Boil, stirring constantly, until the sugar is lightly caramelized. Remove the saucepan from the heat and very carefully (the mixture may splatter) stir in the remaining water. Pour the syrup into 6 ovenproof custard cups.

To prepare the flan, preheat the oven to 350°F/180°C. Whisk together the whole eggs and egg yolks in a medium bowl. Whisk in the milk, sugar, and lemon zest. Pour the egg mixture into the custard cups, dividing evenly. Put the custard cups in a shallow roasting pan. Pour boiling water into the pan to come halfway up the sides of the custard cups. Bake for 30 minutes until a knife inserted in the custard comes out clean. Remove the custard cups from the pan and let cool completely. To serve, unmold the custards onto shallow dessert dishes. ↶

Helado De Vainilla Con Salsa Caliente De Plátano

Vanilla Ice Cream with Hot Banana Sauce

This quick-cooking banana topping for ice cream comes from the Canary Islands, Spain's paradisiacal islands off the coast of North Africa and the only part of Spain with the subtropical conditions necessary to grow bananas. The brown sugar sauce, flavored with lemon zest, nutmeg, and cinnamon, is flamed with *orujo*, a Spanish spirit made from grape skins that is similar to Italian grappa.

Makes 4 servings

- ¼ cup/50 mL unsalted butter
- 3 bananas, peeled and cut into ½-inch/ 1 cm slices
- 2 tbsp/30 mL packed brown sugar
- ¼ tsp/1 mL grated lemon zest
- ¼ tsp/1 mL cinnamon
- ¼ tsp/1 mL freshly grated nutmeg
- 2 tbsp/30 mL *orujo* or grappa
- 2 cups/500 mL good-quality vanilla ice cream
- ¼ cup/50 mL toasted sliced almonds

Melt the butter in a medium skillet over medium heat. Add the bananas, and sprinkle with the sugar, lemon zest, cinnamon, and nutmeg. Simmer for about 2 minutes until the bananas are tender, turning the slices occasionally with a rubber spatula. Standing back, add the *orujo* to the skillet and ignite. When the flames die down, spoon the sauce over the ice cream and sprinkle with the almonds. ⌒

Chocolate Con Churros

Hot Chocolate with Fritters

Churros—the quintessentially Spanish breakfast, afternoon snack, and treat at outdoor fiestas—are typically served with thick rich hot chocolate in which the *churros* may be dunked. In this recipe, the *churros* are transformed into a wonderful dessert.

Makes 6 servings

For hot chocolate:

- ½ cup/125 mL water
- ¼ cup/50 mL granulated sugar
- 1 cup/250 mL finely chopped good-quality semi-sweet chocolate
- ¼ cup/50 mL finely chopped good-quality bittersweet chocolate
- ¼ cup/50 mL whole milk
- 1 tbsp/15 mL good-quality cocoa powder

For churros:

- 1 cup/250 mL water
- 1½ tsp/7 mL mild-flavored extra-virgin olive oil
- ¼ tsp/1 mL kosher or sea salt
- 1 cup/250 mL all-purpose flour
- Mild-flavored olive oil for frying
- Granulated sugar

To prepare the hot chocolate, bring the water and sugar to a boil in a medium saucepan over high heat. Add the semi-sweet and bittersweet chocolates, milk, and cocoa. Reduce the heat to low and cook, stirring constantly with a wooden spoon, until the sauce is thick and smooth, about 5 minutes. Remove the saucepan from the heat.

To prepare the *churros*, bring the water, oil, and salt to a boil in a medium saucepan over high heat. Remove the saucepan from the heat, and add the flour all at once. Stir vigorously with a wooden spoon until the dough forms a smooth ball. Reduce the heat to low and cook for 2 minutes, flattening and turning the dough. Remove the saucepan from the heat and let cool completely.

Preheat the oven to 200°F/93°C. Pour the oil into a large skillet to a depth of 1½ inches/3.5 cm (or better still, use a deep-fryer) and heat over high heat until the oil quickly browns a cube of bread. Meanwhile, spoon the dough into a pastry bag fitted with a ⅜-inch/9 mm star tip (the fluted edge is essential).

Squeeze a few 5-inch/12 cm lengths of dough into the hot oil. Reduce the heat to medium-high and fry for about 20 seconds until the *churros* puff and have barely begun to turn golden. Do not overcook; the *churros* should be crunchy outside and still soft within. Drain on paper towels and keep them warm in the oven until ready to serve. Repeat with the remaining dough to make 24 *churros* in all.

To serve, reheat the chocolate sauce over very low heat and pour into 6 espresso cups placed off-center on 6 dessert plates. Dredge the *churros* in the sugar and arrange 4 on each plate. Serve at once.

Index

Photo Credits

Project Editor: Anna Stancer
Editor: Julia Aitken
Book Design: Benson Ngo
Art Director of Photography: Simon Daley
Index: Ruth Pincoe
Color Separation, Printing and Binding: SNP Leefung, China

Produced by Madison Press Books
Diana Sullada, Art Director
Susan Barrable, Vice President, Finance and Production
Alison Maclean, Associate Publisher
Oliver Salzmann, President and Publisher